MAY GOD BLESS ALL
YOU DO IN HIM.

JAMES 2:26

Thirsty for Christ

The WATER@WORK *Story,*
As Told by Its Founder and the Many That Serve Her

Discussion Guide Included

TABLE OF CONTENTS

Dedications:

I gratefully dedicate this book firstly to Christ Jesus, my Lord and Savior, who loves, empowers and strengthens me. I pray that in some small way this book brings Him glory.

Secondly are two groups of people without whom I cannot imagine what my life would be like. My immediate and extended family, whose love for me and patience with me are both truly incredible. And anyone that has ever uttered a prayer for me during difficult times, or shared praises during all the wonderful times of my life.

Welcome!

In 2006 I had a calling from God. At least I think I did. The path that unfolded had me questioning whether it was real or just a good idea confused by the din of life's background noise. The discerning process wasn't always pretty, but in the end the calling was real and it truly rocked my world.

Initially the biggest issues had to do with time, career, and family. More specifically, it had to do with how I didn't have the time or strength to abandon my comfortable life and follow a still small voice that kept whispering. It was only through prayer and quiet reflection during sleepless nights that I decided to move on the calling. This book is not intended to be overtly motivational, but rather endeavors to relate that story, as well as the ups and downs of many "ordinary" lives that became infused in ministry.

Please note the critical word infused. I'm not referring to a life of dedicated ministry. I didn't stop my life and become a full time missionary, but instead realized that God equipped me in a special way to have talents that He wanted to use for a purpose beyond my selfish interests. Along the way I have been blessed to work with many great folks that were similarly led to share their talents and participate in the ministry dream that God had first laid on my heart, and then on each of theirs.

This book is really about them. The many that decided to give up their precious time with family, friends and every recreational activity one could think of to help build something pretty special. Their tireless efforts conducted almost entirely while balancing full

1

time jobs and full time family responsibilities were simply too inspiring to not write about.

The net result of all the effort was a humble little ministry called Water@Work. This mustard seed of a ministry grew to eventually radically alter the paradigms of traditional non-profit organizations and the lives of tens of thousands in desperate need. Where she has been planted throughout the rural Dominican Republic the gospel is reaching new hearts, great health extends to the residents, and waterborne disease is a thing of the past. Uniquely, a model has been developed that ensures true sustainability for many generations. All of these developments will be fully discussed in this book.

It is truly difficult to not write solely about Water@Work because God has done a mighty work through her.

Along the way a great deal was learned, mostly the hard way, about the realities of starting a mission from nothing but a calling. Because virtually all of us at Water@Work have business and for-profit company experiences, the uniqueness of the non-profit world needed learning and addressing.

We will investigate the many business practices that were incorporated into the non-profit world of ministry to help it be as professional and accountable as possible. Indeed, Water@Work is a melting pot of business executives, professionals, home-makers and persons from every aspect of life imaginable, driven to bring their particular gifts to the mix. I am confident you will see that the lessons learned and discussed herein can be easily correlated to any mission or non-profit organization you may already serve through.

So the goal of this book is to simply tell the story of a special entrepreneurial non-profit organization, the people that built her, and the beautiful people she serves. During its discourse, my prayer is that you see yourself in these servants. No matter what you do for a living, want to do, or dream of doing, there is a ministry out there that can use your help. You will see that you can participate meaningfully while still living the life you enjoy or desire for yourself and your family.

Everyone has a different point where that lies. The lifestyle one chooses for themselves will not be debated herein. We will instead leave that to you and God. What we will discuss is how ordinary people, from the unemployed to millionaires, were able to come together to serve and glorify our Lord.

I have always been struck by the responsibility we face as twenty-first century Americans and disciples of Christ. We were born to the wealthiest country in world history, experienced the finest education in world history, have access to best technology in world history, and for what? Why were our souls given these bodies here and now if not to utilize the resources we have available to radically spread the love of our Savior? Comparing the impact we can have with that of a person just a hundred years ago or so is staggering. This is a special time and you are a special person in its midst.

Each chapter of this book focuses on a perspective of Water@Work throughout its inception and development, as well as a person critically involved at that time. Each chapter starts with a biblical reference that speaks to the topic of the chapter, and then proceeds with the body of the work, a life lesson learned, and a few paragraphs from the person of focus in the chapter in their own words. My challenge to you as you read this book is to somehow see yourself in the characters you will meet here, and then find a great ministry to insert yourself into. Or if you are a glutton for challenge, maybe you'll be led to go off and follow that calling you feel to start something new.

Lastly, I would like to thank you for your purchase of this book. All profits from its sales are being donated to Water@Work. By just purchasing this book, you have brought clean water and the gospel to many families in need!

Bless you, and enjoy!

Introduction

*"God is looking for those with whom He can
do the impossible — what a pity that we plan
only the things that we can do by ourselves."*
A. W. Tozer

Water@Work has developed into a very impactful endeavor.
According to the Dominican Republic Ministry of Public Health, it is
the largest NGO (non-governmental organization) currently
providing water solutions in the country. Not exactly the big fish in a
small pond, but at least a good sized minnow in a large puddle.

Irrespective of size, many tens of thousands of ultra-poor
Haitian refugees and rural Dominicans are now blessed with ample
clean water, good health, and access to the Gospel of Christ.
Importantly, these blessings have been accomplished through a truly
self-sustaining model that also provides significant monies for
community development, and all without any additional revenue
infusions from the ministry or other organization. The key to this
success has been the creation of church businesses in places where
commerce simply doesn't exist, as well as faithful tutelage and
mentoring.

But before jumping into this story of the ministry's inception,
growth and incredible cast of players that is this book, it would be
prudent to spend a few moments on the global water crisis. Even
though many are aware that there is a water crisis in the world, most
would be shocked to learn it is considered by experts as the greatest
single crisis to impact humanity.

In January of 2015, the World Economic Forum released its annual
Global Risks report. It canvassed the knowledge of over 900 leading
experts and decision makers from across the globe to assess, in the report's
own words, "the perceived impact and likelihood of 28 prevalent global

risks over a 10-year time frame." The results of that survey and analysis cemented the following acknowledgement of what has been generally supposed.

TOP 10 GLOBAL RISKS IN TERMS OF IMPACT

1. **Water Crises**
2. Spread of infectious diseases
3. Weapons of mass destruction
4. Interstate conflict
5. Failure of climate-change adaptation
6. Energy price shock
7. Critical information infrastructure breakdown
8. Fiscal crises
9. Unemployment or underemployment
10. Biodiversity loss and ecosystem collapse

One fact hampering efforts to mitigate the impact is that it takes on different personas in different parts of the world. For example, in Africa the issue is primarily finding water, so the solution gravitates towards digging wells and boreholes. By contrast, in the developing countries of the western hemisphere, one can generally find ample water but the issue is serious bacterial contamination.

Worse, in the more advanced of these countries that practice modern farming, chemicals like pesticides and herbicides are now contributing to an actual poisoning of the water. Basically, one solution does not fit all. Considerably different remedies are required to economically deliver healthy water to particular populations based on where one is working.

From a global perspective, the following are a few commonly recognized statistics you may already be aware of.

- Nearly 1 billion people lack access to clean water.
- 1.6 billion people live in areas where there is water, but they can't afford to drink it.
- 90% of sewage produced in underdeveloped countries is discharged untreated into water bodies.

- Over 50% of the hospital beds worldwide are occupied by someone with water-borne disease.
- 80% of all sickness worldwide is related to contaminated water.
- Diarrhea killed more children in the last decade than all armed conflicts since World War II.
- More children die from dirty water every year than war, malaria, HIV/AIDS and traffic accidents combined.

Here are a few statistics that are less known:

- On average, a child dies from water-related illnesses about every seven seconds, or about the time it took to read this bullet.
- 84% of water-related deaths are from children 14 and under.
- The average child who drinks dirty water regularly will have over 1,000 parasites in their body.
- In just the Dominican Republic where Water@Work serves, over 1.2 million children lack access to affordable clean water.

Arguably the worst statistic of all is that an estimated 75% of the Dominican Republic population has no relationship with Jesus Christ! If one wants to imagine the things that make God cry, lack of access to His gospel and clean water must surely be right up there at the top of the list.

Water@Work is the story of a different and unique approach to countering these horrific facts. It represents a radically different model for its operations and delivery of service. It is a model based on exceptional technology, a truly sustainable solution for generations, community development and mentoring, and accountability at every level.

But while Water@Work was just a glimmer in the Almighty's eye, I was the owner of a failing software business that needed a huge miracle that never came. The end of my business took a couple of very painful years because I simply wouldn't give up. So while struggling with how my family and the families of our employees would make it through another month, as well as working through the shame of failure, He turned my life around.

Just before the company met its ultimate demise, I was able to find a young investor to assume the operations and keep all the employees. I even received a small amount of money that helped stabilize our family's financial predicament. Yes, the air actually did smell sweeter, and it seemed as if thousands of pounds were lifted off my back. A huge blessing indeed!

It was during this time, just after the worry and humiliation of that failing enterprise, that He introduced me to the world's water crisis and the water business. With a lot of help from a lot of very smart people, we were able to launch a new company that built portable water purification systems that could clean virtually any water from just solar power. Within the first year we were very successful and life was back on track.

Time to get comfortable again and breathe a bit deeper…

Part 1

Who Needs a Road Map?

TOM FLAIM

1. Life is Good

"Come, follow me," Jesus said, "and I will make you fishers of men." At once they left their nets and followed him.

Matthew 4:18

Have you ever been amazed that, when looking back, you see the hand of God clearly and resolutely during the times you really needed Him? With 20/20 hindsight we thank Him for walking next to us - and most times protecting us from us. One great blessing from following Christ is the knowledge that if we are acting in His will the challenges we encounter become tools for honing us into His likeness. Of course, in the heat of battle the soldier never sees the general's acts of strategy done for the interests of achieving the mission of ultimate victory. We just try and get by while the greater battle plays out at a pay grade way, way, way above ours.

And then there are other times when God sort of smacks you upside the head and says pretty clearly that He has a plan for you and you need to pay attention. I would like to say that when my number was drawn and He spoke to me, I recognized it immediately and jumped to His service. Yes, that would be nice to say. Unfortunately, my thick head was filled with the business of life and I didn't quite feel the heavenly smack.

Perhaps your life isn't that different from mine and you too are so busy you can't imagine working in serious service for our Lord, let alone a calling. Or maybe you feel you have time but aren't utilizing it in a way that seems both satisfying to you and glorifying to God.

I too have been in this place. The ride is going pretty well and life, or at least wholesale segments of time, get switched to auto-pilot. The important thing here is to challenge these time commitments to see if they represent the best you have to offer with your life. Even during these times though, one typically feels the rut they find themselves in takes all their time. How many of us can honestly say we don't feel regularly stressed?

In truth, everyone fills up the 10,080 minutes we get each week doing "things". By the very nature of carrying out these things we seem to live in perpetual motion. I believe many people succumb to this; far too many people seemingly never have enough time for anything new for one reason or another. The resulting general state of tiredness from putting out one fire after another, or the routine of living in routine, seems to permeate all social and economic strata.

And yet any figure one admires, respects, or studies has achieved their accomplishments with the same limited amount of minutes in their week.

Why do you hasten to remove anything which hurts your eye, while if something affects your soul you postpone the cure until next year?
- Horace

But maybe on occasion you felt, as I did, a little nudge that made you stop and think. Perhaps it was a subtle moment when you felt like you should be involved in something that touched your heart. My personal experience was that even among the busyness and distractions, I had a sense that there was something out there that I had been created for; there was some activity that was bigger than I could rationalize at the time. God certainly was working in my life, just as He works in all our lives, to prepare us for Godly "things" that most never would have imagined.

You Did What?

Before I recognized God calling on me, I stayed fairly driven to succeed in all the usual ways. The success of our water company, for which I was incredibly grateful, only led to more nightly and weekend work sessions. My oldest son developed a skill for goal keeping in hockey. So, in my desire to be a good dad, I became a coach and then Head Coach of his team. My other son became an accomplished bassist and we never missed a performance. Even at church there was evening Bible study, mission team involvement, and social get-togethers. Nearly every free minute seemed taken by one worthwhile endeavor or another.

None of this was bad, mind you. I didn't have any particularly destructive or distracting tendencies like excessive drinking or socializing. No "guy's nights out" or large chunks of time spent watching sports or playing video games all the time. Even though I loved to golf, I nearly never played on weekends so I could maximize the time I had with the kids.

The result was a life that was far too busy to hear the specific calling that God wanted me to *focus* on. We'll explore this malady further in the next chapter, but for now let's meet a friend that took a different path.

Actually, we started out as anything but friends. Erven Kimble was in fact a significant business competitor of mine. We were in engineering sales and had an almost Mohamad Ali / Joe Frazier relationship. Rather than in the ring, though, we duked it out in the world of corporate computer system sales. It certainly wasn't as glamorous as a boxing ring on an international stage, but the competition was just as real. And, as can happen among competitors in a small arena, we became good friends. What I didn't know at the time was that while we were going back and forth trying to win the next deal, he was in seminary at night preparing for a shepherd's life.

One day I called Erv to tell him I was leaving corporate America to start my own business. Knowing what a great competitor and professional he was, I offered him an equity position and opportunity to join me as a partner. That's when he told me he was moving on as well; he was retiring from his position at the ripe old age of forty. While we were both handsomely rewarded for our work, there was no way he could have pulled off retirement so young. So with a good bit of not-so-gentle prodding, we spoke at length about how he had "been called" to be a pastor. He reluctantly rejected the opportunity to be part owner of a very promising business so he could become a pastor. At the time I had not yet committed my life to Christ and hadn't been in a church for a couple decades. I listened like a good friend should, and walked away with the absolute certainty he was crazy.

After another dozen years or so, I was in his town and looked him up. We caught up and laughed a lot. Erv has a laugh that is both infectious and bold, and one that's impossible to ignore or deflect. I shared with him my recent decision to place my faith and life in the hands of Jesus. After some good hearted ribbing about the odds of such an event, he described his new life in detail, namely the challenges, frustrations, disappointments and reduced living standard of the life he now led. He also said he had never been so happy, satisfied, fulfilled, or driven in his entire life.

My friend Erv had moved from successful professional to humble servant. And I still couldn't understand it fully. We were living the American Dream and had spent many years living the good life and racking up earthly treasures. We weren't bad guys, just focused on career and family. Winning the next deal used to be what drove us, but he now had a much bigger vision for his life. He was no longer satisfied with running a corporate sales team. He got near the top of the corporate ladder and discovered that the next rung wasn't another career promotion, but rather a *life* promotion. He emphatically told me that he hadn't lost anything, but gained more than he could describe.

Uh, yeah. Thanks. So with no need for tact among friends, I told him I was glad there are folks like him, but not for me. Still, I was kind of feeling a little something that was wholly unfamiliar to me at that point in my life.

Perhaps you are reading this book under similar circumstances. You can feel or sense that you should be more heavily invested in ministry, but life just keeps putting up roadblocks. Maybe yours isn't necessarily like Erv's, where it's all or nothing. Maybe there's a way to serve Christ in critical ministry while still raising a family, enjoying a career, and happily moving along with your life. If so, I pray you take comfort and impact from this book. It endeavors to show that through the lives of ordinary folks like yourself, and the anointing from an awesome God, a humble mustard seed of effort can truly grow into a mighty tree of life for many.

But first, we need to get back to Erv and the unpaved path.

Who has Time for Missions?

My conversations with Erv, as well as the finer points of faith that I was absorbing through regular worship service and bible studies started me thinking differently. I was now looking for a way I could express my enthusiasm in a constructive and tangible way. Like any great church, the one our family attended provided many ways to channel this desire. Soon I was joining other professionals and neighbors, serving both locally at some great charities and within the church. We all freely shared with each other how we got that special "feel good" that can only come from service work.

> *Even the slightest movement towards the things God cares for will be recognized by Him and turned into giant strides.*

Making time for kingdom work was difficult at first, but it became easier as I chose to make it a priority. I constantly reminded myself that while I still had the same responsibilities to my family and career, I now had another significant responsibility to God that really overarched everything else. Quite simply I needed to share his love as fully as possible while still being responsible to job and family.

The First Taste of Mission

Not long after my somewhat confusing visit with Erv, the church our family attended announced it was going to have a mission trip to the Dominican Republic. The trip was open to anyone that wanted to go. For some reason known only to God, I turned to my wife Sue and whispered that it would be good for us and the kids to go. She agreed, although we really had no idea what we were doing or signing up for.

This became stunningly apparent as we planned our schedules for the trip. We figured we could spend the week with the team working, and then stay another week at a resort as a vacation. We would do some good work in some dirty place and then relax and enjoy comforts that exceeded even what we had at home. We really had no idea.

But in our ignorance we did just that. We found a beautiful all-inclusive resort with a nearly endless pristine beach and free-flowing food and drinks. It was the perfect plan. We do a little of God's work, and then relax and enjoy a well-deserved vacation.

Because it is too embarrassing to come back to later, I will provide a spoiler alert. We did spend the second week in the lap of luxury, and it was certainly awkward. I kept thinking back on the week of service that changed my life and would have rather gone back and served more or just come home early. Not that there is anything wrong with a nice vacation, but our time in service trumped it.

But that's enough for now. In a coming Chapter, we'll fully discuss that first time in the international mission field and its impact on all of us.

God at the Driver's Wheel

One thing I think I did get right, and for those counting this is likely the only thing, was my honest conversation with God when I finally gave in and agreed to His Lordship over my life. After a long road of studying various religions and philosophies, the Gospel of Christ Jesus was the only one that truly made sense to me. My faith journey has had many bumps and embarrassing moments (witness the last few paragraphs), but the maturing process of the Holy Spirit is a beautiful and fantastic thing. There have been thousands of books written on why but for me, the change in my life for the better is incalculable.

If you are reading this book and have not had that conversation and yielded your life to Him, I pray you stop reading right now and do it. It is far more important than anything you will read in here. But as you will see when this book unfolds, God had a plan for me to do a mighty work for Him…and He has a plan for you.

It may be something as personal as being the best parent or spouse you can be, or it might lead you on a path to different countries and experiences. There can be no doubt, however, that you will change and you will make a bold difference for Him. You may not recognize it now, but you will be a key to help establish His Kingdom.

So let's get back to the issue of finding time for God's work and meet everyday folks that were used by God to be critical pieces of one particular mission.

Life Lesson 1:
Even a wretch like me can experience amazing grace and make a difference.

From Pastor Kimble to you:

I remember the times in my life when I was moved to make serious commitments as a servant of Christ. Oftentimes, I would wonder about my destiny as a servant. Usually, we understand the word "destiny" as a conclusion; a destination or place that is reached. I believe our destiny is more of a journey, an excursion, or a voyage.

When our providence is in relationship with Jesus as Lord, we are compelled to take on the same journey or path that Jesus took. It is a journey that leads to the cross. After all, the servant is not greater than the master. Regardless of our unique circumstances, each of us that are called to serve Him will inevitably have to emulate His destiny as well.

In seeking your destiny, God will tear down what we have built out of our own knowledge and self-reliance. But through brokenness, God will establish Himself as our lone source of Life. Isn't it a wonderful thing that our Creator allows Tom and me to both share in the glory of His beloved Son?

2. Marginal Importance

"I know that there is nothing better for people than to be happy and to do good while they live. That each of them may eat and drink, and find satisfaction in all their toil—this is the gift of God."

Ecclesiastes 3:12-13

Making time available for any activity is hard. We are a people and society that rewards being busy and it leads to a feeling that we don't have extra time available for other worthy activities. The reality is very different, although it may necessitate some changed perceptions. One way to think of it is like a margin. Margins can mean anything from the spaces at the edge of this page to margins of safety.

Margins here, though, may best be thought of in financial terms. The Random House College Dictionary defines *margin* as "the difference between the cost and the selling price." From the margin, a business derives its profit. Generally the more built in margin, the more stable and healthy the business. Our personal lives aren't very different than this. In this corollary we should first assume that our "cost" is the time we need for all the activities that are core to our health, responsibilities, and interests. The selling price can then be thought of as the total time in any period. With these assumptions the time margin is the difference between the time we have and the time we need for core activities.

Many times in business one cannot raise the price due to market factors. Similarly, we cannot really increase the amount of time God has planned for our earthly existence. The only way to increase our time margin is to reduce the time spent on core activities. This can be very difficult and takes some sincere hard looks at how we spend the time we have. Do we really need to feel so stressed all the time, even on worthy activities?

> Increasing our margin of time is important to service. One cannot feel they are cramming yet another activity into an already packed schedule. Dr. Richard Swenson has written an entire book on this topic aptly titled *Margin*. He explains: *"Marginless is being asked to carry a load five pounds heavier than you can lift; margin is a friend to carry half the burden. Marginless is not having the time to finish the book you're reading on stress; margin is having the time to read it twice."*

Speaking on this thought, James Bryan Smith in his book *The Good and Beautiful God*, furthers the discussion by stating that *"The number one spiritual sickness of our day is hurry sickness… When we lack margin in our lives we become tired and lonely and joyless, which seems to invite temptation."*

Of course knowing and understanding the issue does not resolve the issue. There are many ways to increase the margin in one's life, but they need to be conscious and deliberate. Mr. Smith further states that there is a simple but very difficult solution to the issue by *"just saying no. Say no to anything that is not absolutely necessary to the well-being of your soul or the welfare of others"*. At first this seems a mighty high ledge to climb onto. However, it really comes down to looking hard at everything that needs time and eliminating unessential ones. One can also:

- Defer a task or activity to someone else. Many times this will help them flourish through the new responsibility.
- Reduce one's amount of television time. Is taking time to watch the news while also reading it off your smart phone or computer really necessary?
- Get up fifteen minutes earlier in the morning..
- Go to bed fifteen minutes later.

- Engage yourself in *one* church activity that you are passionate about and let others grow in their service to the church by assuming those activities you are not passionate about.
- Become a *facilitator* instead of *doer*.
- Look for others in your spheres of influence that are ready for growth and *delegate*.
- Don't check and reply to emails after reasonable hours.
- Make the effort to determine and quantify what robs you of margin.

How Much is the Right Amount?

I'm certain that as you think it through you will come up with many ways to increase your time margin that makes the most sense for you. Unlike time margin, which is a very important contemporary principle, tithing is an Old Testament principle that is also essential to contemporary discipleship. The need for followers of Christ to give back is critical to our faithfulness. Wouldn't it be fair that God would want to see us faithful in simple acts such as this before entrusting us with activities important to *Him*? As humans, we might wrongfully see this as a quid pro quo. Rather than heavenly deal-making though, it seems only fair to me that God should get some assurance that we can be trusted before actually trusting us. If you have raised children, then as they grew you likely followed a similar path.

Carried further, I remember a time when I was blessed to be a partner of a company that sought to grow significantly. After making sure that all employees were being fairly compensated, we gave away 10% of the company profits to various charities that represented our customer base. It was a way of not only being faithful to God, but also a way of giving back to the community that had enabled our success.

We see similar results with our personal resources: how could we expect God to bless our company with exceptional growth if we could not demonstrate faithfulness with our company resources?

This of course would never work with large or publicly held companies. But for small business executives, take the same step of faith in your business that you take personally and watch what God does!

I "cry" less about my personal situations when I focus on the things God cries about. All the issues and distractions of life become secondary to the mission God lays on your heart.

I decided the best way to resolve my time margin issue was to be a little more inclusive on the meaning of tithing. If I release to God the financial tithe He asks for both personally and through the company he blessed me to steward, then why shouldn't I commensurately tithe my time?

While not too scientific, here's what worked for me. I tried to determine my free time by removing the time committed to all my necessary activities from the finite time I had, such as:

- 11 hours per day for work (including drive time)
- 8 hours for sleep
- 1 hour for dinner
- 2 hours per night on average for other obligations like coaching my son's hockey team, driving my other son to guitar lessons, regular bible study, etc.

That only left about 2 hours per day free that I tended to fill up with a list too long to list. Then the weekends offered additional free time that I calculated at 8 hours per day, providing exceptions for church attendance, family visits and, of course, football season. All in all, with 10 hours during the week and another 16 during the weekend, I figured on having 26 hours per week available.

If you've not had the pleasure, this is how an engineer like me thinks and gets to decisions. Giving a minimum tithe of at least 10%

of my time for God's work meant I should be increasing my time margin at least 3 hours per week (yes, God appreciates it when you round up). This still left a reasonable remaining 23 hours for all the other "stuff". I'm sure your analysis could have different obligations and allocations, but the end result would likely be similar.

As time went on, I shifted priorities to make sure I gave at least three hours per week to a couple different charities. I soon realized that I had even more time than I had calculated. Significantly, the stuff filling my remaining 23 hours didn't seem as important or fulfilling as it once did. It was clearly not as important as the work I was allocating to the three tithe hours. My time margin grew all by itself from my love for service, and I found myself spending far more time on Godly work.

Like many others that have travelled a similar path, I learned that service work and a desire to tangibly share Christ's love became integral to my personal core. Through the power of the Holy Spirit, everything I did during my daily routine began to radiate from this core. In essence, one doesn't have to add another category to life that needs to be "forced" into everything else, or added to the list of everything else. Rather, it just becomes part of who you are and you find plenty of time for everything.

From this humble start at regular service work I began to yearn for a special effort that would take advantage of my skill sets. I really wanted to feel like I was truly living within His will with everything I had to offer.

Every Coin Has Two Sides

The flip side to the desire of working free time into a busy schedule is those with extra time already available. I grant you nobody feels they have extra time. It would be nearly impossible to find anyone that would say they have extra hours each week that are just wasted. This is primarily because of our tendency to fill a vacuum. Have you moved into a new home with extra closet space? It will be filled up very shortly. Have a night with nothing to do?

You'll probably use that time to discover the new television series everyone is talking about. You get the idea.

We do everything we can to limit this situation in children and adolescents. Keeping them "busy" reduces the opportunities for them to get into trouble. I certainly wouldn't argue with that and have employed this concept in the rearing of my own children. However, when as adults it creeps into virtually every aspect and every minute of life, it might be a good time to re-assess one's priorities. Many studies have been conducted on this and conclude that we are nearly all guilty in this regard. If we have free time, we fill it.

As a young man, I was as much a product of this ailment as anyone. I did not marry until nearly thirty years of age. During this time of being single and (mostly) free from financial or any other type of real burden, I had a ridiculous amount of free time. I became an armchair authority on virtually all sports and filled huge amounts of time watching games and growing knowledgeable about the current condition of a great many teams and players. Again, there is nothing wrong with being a sports fan, but I could have easily satiated my love of sport and still given God a little something. Today, it could easily be video games, social media or any number of contemporary time killers.

The sad truth in this is that it is the young that typically have the energy and freedom to really make a difference. Most importantly, they do not generally carry the baggage of those with a few more miles on the tread. Their creative approach to problem solving and understanding of new communications technologies can be vital to any non-profit. As a ministry or non-profit leader, harnessing these energies and skills infuses new life into any effort. If you are the one with the time, you are badly needed. A great start is to simply identify something you are passionate about then asking them "*How can I help?*"

Do People Really Do This?

I can easily come up with many examples of people that have increased their time margins to answer the bell in what they are called to do. I'm also sure you can think of people in your life that seemed to "all of a sudden" be very involved in some activity or non-profit. And then there are those that just always seem to be able to work in time to their busy schedules when they feel it matters.

Pastor Larry Wood is a mentor and good friend that held this ability, and was also responsible for my formative Christian development. Larry has been retired for some years now, but was the founding Pastor of our church and oversaw its growth to a sizable congregation before retiring. The first time I met Larry was after attending my first worship service at his then somewhat young church with about three hundred members.

A church that size has many needs from its pastor, and ours was no different. Larry's life was a conglomeration of everything anyone could imagine. I never knew how he held it all together. A typical day might include sermon development, staff meetings, session meetings, budget meetings, nighttime bible study, visits to the hospital, senior living center, the children's day school, community programs, time with his wife, visits with his adult children and any other humanly possible thing.

But after a few services I had the opportunity to meet him privately and we spoke at length. I told him of my busy life that included a growing business, two young boys with more energy than an atomic bomb, and a particular problem that was really bothering me. At the time I was the President of the Board of Directors of a Habitat for Humanity Affiliate in the Atlanta area. The Affiliate had only built an average of one home every two years and my Board was unsure of how to grow the organization.

The Affiliate I had stepped up to help with had some very significant structural issues and I was spending a lot of time trying to determine a path forward. Larry didn't flinch when he simply asked: "how can I help?" Never one to be shy in accepting help, I told him

I could use his perspective on our Board. Larry then joined our Board and proceeded to help me turn the Affiliate around in just a half year. Soon we were building several houses per year and the patient was stabilized.

That was when Larry did something unexpected. He quit. We were all set for continued growth and set some heady goals when he just quit! It was then that I learned the real secret to time margin. He recognized that his capabilities were no longer *critical* to our success and he wanted to free his time margin for other needs. The word critical is, well, critical. He could have stayed on longer, like I had hoped for, but he knew when to pull out and help elsewhere.

This first-hand exposure to a master doer was invaluable in understanding how to accomplish much for the Kingdom while still meeting all the familiar obligations everyone has. If you haven't already done it, I would highly recommend the exercise of determining what is truly *critical* to you and your service to God, and then exiting from all others. Your time margin, as well as sanity, might just increase significantly and you will be freer to fully execute His plan in your life.

Life Lesson 2:
Knowing when to leave an endeavor is critical to managing time margin.

From Pastor Larry to you:

Tom is much too generous with his affirmation of my management skills. It is true I did "quit" his agency when I felt I was no longer needed. It was evident that Tom had things well under control and the Habitat for Humanity Affiliate was beginning to flourish. It was a joy to watch house after house completed and those in need have a new home. It was a privilege to work with Tom and observe his total commitment to the agency's ministry.

There have been, during my 45 years of ministry, a half dozen agencies on whose boards of directors I served. When I realized a board was more interested in preserving the status quo or was taking the ministry in a direction I could not support, I resigned. The same is true for those treading water or not interested in addressing ethical issues. I carefully watched for over-extending. I also avoided national boards due to lack of time and financial resources, but mostly because I considered my local responsibilities the priority.

My God-given time was a precious gift and I want to be a good and faithful steward of that gift.

Tom has provided some very valuable insights into our use of our limited time. We would do well to pay attention to his prized suggestions.

3. It All Began With a Mission Trip

*He said to them, "Go into all the world and
preach the good news to all creation."*

Mark 16:15

It is pretty amazing how small the world has become. Not too many years ago there were only international missionaries—intrepid folks of strong body and soul that spent their lives in faraway places with strange and unknown cultures. We are all actually products of missionaries and owe our message of salvation to their selflessness and willingness to leave everything and everyone they loved to spread the Gospel. Starting with the woman at the well and moving on to Paul and then the apostles, if it weren't for people of God to have the courage to step out of their comfort zones, there is a distinct likelihood few of us would have the relationship with Christ required to ensure our salvation.

In more recent times, God's calling of missionaries has not abated. Many have dedicated their lives and continue to do so, giving up nearly every comfort so that people in the far reaches of the planet could have the Godly relationship we all cherish. However, in only the past few decades a new type of missionary has emerged.

The missionary that works all year in every form and fashion of labor in the *developed* world, only to leave for a bit and experience the blessing of spreading Christ's love in the *developing* world. No longer is it necessary to give up one's entire life and leave everything. Now it is easy for tradesmen, factory workers, doctors, clerks, students, and just about anyone else to experience serving Christ in the developing world.

A national survey in 2006 determined that 2.1% of church members of all denominations (1.6 million people) had been on a short-term mission trip in the past year. I'm sure in the subsequent years the number has grown even larger. It would be hard to find a Christian church in the developed world today that does not offer what is typically a week long mission trip somewhere. Through construction, local vacation bible school, medical work, or any number of useful endeavors, many organizations stand ready to facilitate such a trip with little more than a decision to do it.

When guided by the Holy Spirit, we realize that "our community" means "the world", and our desire to serve God helps us get there.

One would also be hard pressed to find anyone that has been on one of these short term mission trips that has not come back home changed by the experience. Let me be as direct as possible here: ***Every person in the developed world should absolutely do everything possible to take a short term international mission trip as soon as you can.*** The remainder of this entire book could discuss nothing but the blessings of participating in just such a trip.

However, we shall instead continue with the incredible way God used my first short term mission trip to ultimately bring the Gospel, good health, and community development to the at-risk population of an entire country. So let's just leave this here with the oft-quoted Nike slogan "Just Do It," and move on.

Our First Mission Trip

All international mission trips, and particularly one's first, have a life of their own. It generally starts with a great feeling of anticipation and practical concerns:

- What will we see?
- What the food will be like?

- What should we bring?
- Will we be able to communicate?

And then there are the prayers:

- I pray I can make some difference.
- I pray God speaks to me through the experience.
- I pray I don't get sick from drinking the water or eating the ice.
- I pray I can get out from under the pile of work I'll come back to.

But all those concerns pretty much end as soon as you enter the country. All those anxious moments transition with the inevitable chaos one immediately experiences, and it just goes on from there. Thoughts shift to new local experiences, such as how it's possible to fit five vehicles abreast on a road clearly designed for two lanes, or what the exchange rate is on the money, and why it takes thousands of the local currency to just get a bottle of water.

Pretty soon though, you get into a flow and the excitement and experience just continue. On my first mission trip, which happened to be to the Dominican Republic, our host was Pastor Pedro Kery Johnson. Pedro is best described as an ambitious man of God with faith and dreams the size of the island. Pastor Pedro first introduced us to typical life in a Dominican city because we stayed at his mission house in the small but busy town of Barahona.

Barahona lies in a desert area close to the border with Haiti. As the trip was in the dead of summer, every day approached or exceeded 100 degrees and the heat only relented slightly into the evening. To try and get some breeze and cool off, we all had the particular treat of sleeping on the mission house roof. We moved some mattresses up there and settled in for a good night's sleep under the clear skies and star-lit night. That is, until the roosters crowed all night, the dogs barked all night, the motor scooters scooted all night, and the local bar blasted music all night. Our first morning was marked with a clear resignation that there was no way we could ever get any sleep for the rest of the week.

Missions are not a recruitment project for God's labor force. It is a liberation project from the heavy burdens and hard yokes of other gods.

- John Piper

The next day we were told we would be re-building a part of a local church that had been severely damaged by an earthquake. Awesome! This was a real chance to accomplish a tangible goal in only the way that a goal driven American could appreciate. We were going to achieve something.

Only my boys, who accompanied my wife and me on the trip, understood that true experiential value came from relationships and not accomplishments. Our youngest, at thirteen, was busily playing with other local kids and having a blast. Although they couldn't speak each other's language, he showed immediately that he liked them and discovered that they weren't that much different at all. Our oldest was sixteen and he was constantly busy asking the local young adults every sort of question one could imagine and displaying a respect-based curiosity that was magnetic. None of us could wait to get started!

Everyone Loves Batey 7

Pastor Pedro did a great job of getting us out to our work site. We were allowed to ride in the back of an open pickup truck that literally rode over goat trails and extremely rough segments of dirt that are euphemistically called roads. The village we finally arrived at could have been mistaken for any one of the dozens that we drove by.   It was very small and nearly engulfed by the seemingly continuous sugar cane fields that cover the island.

Our team was tasked with tearing down a six inch thick concrete wall and replacing it with a new one. It should have been a piece of cake, only we didn't have any tools. Instead of any number of devices that would have completed the task in less than a day, we were handed small 16oz. claw hammers and left to our work. We pounded and pounded until we couldn't move our arms anymore. Then as a sure sign of providence, God blessed us with a sledge hammer. Not exactly the power equipment we craved, but a step up for sure.

Over the course of the week, the team tore down walls, broke up the concrete floor, and formed and poured new concrete columns and walls. Despite minimal tools and mixing all the concrete by hand, we generally had a great time. Sweating alongside the local residents that came out to help in every way they could, we got to really know them and develop friendships that last to this day. Their gentle smiles and acts of appreciation said more than the words they spoke that we couldn't fully understand.

During work breaks, we gave the endless tide of children piggy back rides that, no matter how many we offered, were never enough. Exhausted and nearly oblivious at the end of each day, we would walk the batey and smile, shake hands, and pray for as many residents as we could. Suffice it to say that none of us ever heard another scooter or rooster at night and we slept like babies.

A single thought resonated with all of us, though: how could people with virtually nothing get up every day and survive?

Chaggy Makes it Personal

While Pastor Pedro oversaw group logistics and transportation, he made sure that a young man named Antonio Feliz Gomez, or Chaggy as everyone knows him, saw to everything else we could have needed. Chaggy was our official translator, but quickly became a close friend. Since he wasn't too many years older than my oldest son, he hit it off with the boys immediately and they still remain very close.

Chaggy's story begins with a Dominican family struggling with not having enough to eat and too many mouths to feed. Because he was the oldest, Chaggy had to leave his family and live on the streets and in the parks from the age of twelve. Like many in this poor country, Chaggy primarily begged and shined shoes as a means of existing. But as God has a plan for everyone, he bumped into Pastor Pedro and was welcomed into his mission house. There, Pedro taught Chaggy basic English and enrolled him into tourism school.

Unfortunately, the money ran out and Chaggy made his way by being a "Guy Friday" for Pedro. He was responsible for doing whatever the Pastor needed, which was essentially watching after the mission teams that regularly stayed at his Mission House.

Chaggy is a wonderful young man that has an incredible story. He regularly witnesses to many and dreams of being a Pastor. His powerful testimony has brought many to Christ, and his love for everyone is infectious. For all of us on our trip, he made the Dominican story real. In a very tangible way, we were able to relate to life in this harsh environment. His courageous path and rags to (eternal) riches story inspires everyone that meets him. For me personally, it took this very personal person-to-person exchange to realize that I needed to do something to help.

Incredibly, short term mission trips can also become the delivery vehicle for romance. Several years after our trip, a young woman named Denise took a short term mission trip from Boston and met Chaggy. They ultimately fell in love, married, and Chaggy moved to America. I was extremely proud to serve as his Best Man at the wedding.

Chaggy and Denise now reside with their young child Levi in North Carolina. While happy, they dream of moving to the Dominican Republic to pursue their goal of being full time missionaries, and Chaggy has not given up on his personal mission of becoming a pastor in his homeland.

One Particular Blessing

As it happens, I am an engineer and involved in a water purification business. Our customer base is American hospitals and health care facilities where we provide emergency water backup should a facility lose their municipal water supply through natural or man-made disasters. Figuring that we might not have access to clean water the entire time we were in-country, I brought a portable version of the water purification system with us on the trip.

You would have thought we brought gold. At a local cistern that had collected rain water and every form of water disease one could imagine, we purified the water so the team could take **very** frequent water breaks. Within minutes, local women and children from the village started lining up with buckets, pots, pans, or anything else that could store water. We spent the entire week filling every vessel possible with clean safe water for their use.

Our kids also had a great time hosing off the local children in the same way kids in America spend hours playing with a hose in the back yard. Amazing to us was learning from Chaggy and Pedro that for many, this was their first experience with clean water! It was also the very beginning of the ministry that is the focus of this book, as well as the start of a journey that has changed the lives of hundreds of thousands of lives in the Dominican Republic, and hundreds of servants in this country.

This incredible and very personal experience was my pivotal moment. I was finally in a place and time where God's call to me was a scream I could no longer ignore.

Life Lesson 3
Put yourself in a position and place for God to use you, and He will.

From Chaggy to you:

Of all the things that somebody can have any place in the world, clean water is the most important. God made it first and made it to be the source of life in nature. Jesus himself used the water from the well with the Samaritan women to explain that He is the water of life. This ministry provides not only the physical water the woman at the well needed and that we all need as well, but then most importantly, the living water that we all absolutely need for our salvation.

The people in the Dominican Republic do not have much, but I can testify boldly that God always provides. There were many, many days when I went without any food or water. It was only my faith in a providing God that saw me through it.

I have spent many days in the bateys ministering to the people there. They actually had less than me. For them, clean water and a meal are true luxuries. I have seen with my own eyes how the blessing of clean water can change much in these villages and result in people coming to Christ.

You may not be able to spiritually save somebody, but you are able to make a difference that will help another person to be saved.

4. So What Exactly is a Batey?

"For you will always have the poor among you, but you will not always have me."

Matthew 26:11

In the next few years after that first mission trip to the Dominican Republic, I was truly blessed to have traveled internationally, helping those in need of clean water. Through these trips to virtually every corner of the earth, I have learned and matured exponentially. As one might expect, each trip started with trepidation, concern and a reasonable measure of fear. More importantly, each trip ended with me coming home and telling everyone what an unbelievable experience I had.

Unique circumstances and opportunities for growth on every trip yielded enormous leaps forward in my faith journey. For instance:

Ecuador, South America: Here, we worked high in the Andes Mountains close to the Colombian border trying to clean water from a lake that was as foul as anything I have ever seen. The area and conditions are a true lesson in how to turn one of the most idyllic places imaginable into a wasteland through fertilizers, herbicides, and pesticides that run off into the water.

While testing to see just how bad the water was, we had to flee from the armed drug lords that regularly came to the villages to "recruit" children to harvest their drug crop. Later we truly tested the quality of our technology by cleaning and drinking the water from the Manchangara River, considered by many the most polluted river in the western hemisphere.

Haiti, Caribbean Sea: Most folks pretty much understand the conditions in Haiti. I have been there several times, but the most memorable was immediately after the great earthquake of 2010. This 7.0 quake and its after-shocks left an unimaginable quarter million people perished, and another quarter million injured.

We delivered water purification equipment across Port au Prince and the affected neighboring areas within just days after the quake. Our base of operations was an infectious care hospital that was designed for no more than a hundred people, but that was now serving several thousand. In that specific trip I saw more angels serving God's children than I thought He could have had in heaven.

Kenya, Africa: A twelve hour drive from the nearest major city north across the desert led us to the middle of nowhere. There, we were blessed to preach and introduce Christ to several unreached Bedouin tribes. It was also an opportunity to feel real frustration in that there simply wasn't any water to clean. When what you have to offer is a very efficient way to clean bad water, nothing can be more frustrating than going all that way to realize there simply isn't any water coming from the wells and you really can't help much.

Chicago and Atlanta, North America: Anyone with a heart and eyesight can readily see the need for Christian service in our own country. Prior to my commitment in international water ministry, I was very involved in serving the homeless and building affordable homes for the working poor. While very satisfying, there always seemed to be plenty of workers for this harvest.

In contrast to the United States where nearly all people know of Christ and many times choose apathy or outright rejection, one of the great and unique opportunities in international ministry is meeting fellow human beings that have never heard of Christ. US-based service is indeed very rewarding, but international missions simply offer the opportunity to spread the gospel of Christ to literally millions of people starving for it.

All of my trips led to a deepening relationship with Christ. In addition to the prospect of experiencing people in real need for my two developing passions – clean water and living water – each had struck a chord from different perspectives. However, the one that really *resonated* was my trip to the Dominican Republic.

To resonate requires that every chord work together to make a perfect sound. If even one string is not struck perfectly, the sound may be acceptable and even sound really good to others, but it will not resonate with you.

> *God calls each believer into His service. The best place to hear the call is in His mission field while focused in Christian service and away from daily distractions.*

Something could have gone wrong on the Dominican mission trip at any moment, and it did, but working in the rural Dominican village really hit home for me. It wasn't anything in particular; there were no drug lord chases, earthquake crisis, or technology challenges, but a very real sense that this is what I was being called to do.

The Invisible Poor

In the local Creole dialect, the name "batey" literally translates into "place of suffering". Nobody, not even the government, knows exactly how many bateys there are in the Dominican. Amnesty International estimates the number at 400, but the government doesn't know because they don't count. Not just counting as in numerically, but also count as in concern. The residents of these bateys are considered persona non grata, or persons without a country. While located just an hour or so south of Florida by plane, their plight is virtually unknown in the US.

The problem began back in the 1930's and continues on to the present. The sugar cane companies needed cheap labor to work the fields. They would go to Haiti and elicit workers, people that were obviously eager to have any work at all, and then bring them back to the Dominican by bus. They built company villages, similar to the coal towns of the US in the early twentieth century.

The companies essentially owned every aspect of their life, and the people became virtual slaves to the company. However, when the harvest was complete, they did not bring them back. Instead, they left them there so they would have a ready work force for the following years' work. An agreement by the respective dictators of the two countries at the time actually encouraged this contemporary form of slavery. Bateys like these are referred to as company-owned, and primarily populate the eastern side of the country.

A second type of batey developed in the west, closer to the Haitian border. These bateys arose from Haitians immigrating to avoid political instability, disease, and just for the hope of getting work. While both types of bateys offer very austere living conditions, the non-company bateys are generally considered even more desperate.

To envision these western bateys, picture a hot and oppressing place where the children kick up dust with every barefoot step on the dirt roads. Most shacks that the people live in have large gaps in the roof that lets the occasional rain pour onto the dirt floor.

Life is hard – really hard - and hard in ways we simply cannot fully comprehend. One visitor remarked that she thought it may resemble the conditions the Jews endured during the time of Christ. While I've not yet been blessed to travel to the Holy Land, I can imagine the resemblance.

On a trip to one of these rural non-company bateys, a teammate asked what the unemployment rate was. The local elder responded five. We could not believe that there was only a five percent unemployment rate given the conditions. After some more accurate translating, we learned that a total of five people had a real job! That is five out of the one thousand or so that lived there.

Pause for a second and let that sink in.

The local boys there hope to grow up and at least get some work in the fields. The girls generally make babies or move to the cities for work primarily in prostitution. In 2005, the United Nations Development Program focused its attention on the Dominican bateys:

> *"Haitians live in the country (Dominican Republic) in very precarious conditions of extreme poverty. Furthermore, most of them are undocumented and must face a generally hostile political and social situation ... two thirds of batey inhabitants lack access to a water filtration system and direct access to a river."*

On his CNN television show, aired on December 18, 2006, Anderson Cooper of Anderson Cooper 360 reported that:

> *The old or infirm looked like they were starving. One old man told us he hadn't eaten in four days. Children told us they planted cane in Vicini (the local sugar cane company) fields for three pesos (approximately 3 cents) a row. It takes a half day to plant a row.*

Enter voodoo. And this is not the corner curiosity shop you might experience in New Orleans, but the very real type that controls lives. Many batey residents from Haiti bring with them the belief in this frightening practice that truly confuses people and is a significantly large impediment for people coming to Christ.

Local batey churches struggle mightily against this perversion of religion. Many resist, and through their efforts and the grace of God, progress is being made in the fight against this insidious enemy.

But all is not lost. Moises Sifren is the Senior Administrator of the second largest hospital on the east side of the island. He is incredibly articulate and is fluent in both Spanish and English. Meeting Moises is like being introduced to any professional you might ever happen upon in the United States. He is a committed Christian serving his people with lifesaving medical care, and he is also a former child of a batey. His story, while not typical, illustrates the capacity of batey children to ultimately succeed against incredible odds.

Moises is a living example of Christian love given, and then paid forward "seventy times seven times". He is one of ten children from Haitian parents who met and lived a very typical life in a sugar cane batey. On her tenth pregnancy, his mother developed complications during delivery from high blood pressure. She was very fortunate to be taken to a city hospital for the delivery. Incredibly, the doctors were on strike when she arrived and the hospital was essentially closed.

Soon after she was turned away, the family simultaneously welcomed a new beautiful little girl into the family but then said goodbye to their matriarch as she passed into Paradise. While one would think this bittersweet but ultimately sad tale would end here, God took this injustice and produced a miracle.

The pastor at the batey worked with other pastors to raise awareness for the need of a different kind of hospital that would never turn anyone away. He also made sure Moises had a proper education and mentored him after the loss of his mother. Many dozens of American churches came forward with gifts of financial resources and mission teams to help. The result became the Buen Samaritano Hospital, translated as the Good Samaritan Hospital, a new amazing Christian hospital where Moises currently serves as the Senior Administrator.

Over the last two decades the hospital has grown to care for over 65,000 patients per year, and employs over 400 persons. This is quite astounding considering nearly all the labor to build the facility has come from American mission teams.

Never to be satisfied, the hospital is currently adding a fourth floor and will soon expand its operations and outreach to even greater numbers of the poor. Moises, who eagerly shares his story, is fond of saying that *"I know how big God is because I have seen with my own eyes what He has done here."*

Moises is a living example of how a typical child in the worst of situations can grow to make a huge difference in their community with some help from caring individuals and the blessing of an almighty God.

Hope in a Hopeless Place

While it would be easy to focus on the horrible conditions that these more than 1,000,000 people endure, as well as the many ultra-poor Dominicans in not much better circumstances, that is *not* their story. Rather, theirs is a story of hope and perseverance. The most earnest prayers I have ever heard uttered came from the tiny shacks that serve as churches. It is truly humbling to pray with these wonderful people, knowing that the least among us here in the developed world has far more than any of them.

Most persons that venture into these towns of several thousand see only a dirty, dusty and sometimes scary place. They would define their experience with words like *despair, misery* or *abject poverty*. Coupled with the heat and extremely remote locations, *hell* has also been a descriptive word thrown around by some. However, through our mission work we had the opportunity to really get to know the people in a deeper way. We listened to their struggles and dreams. We prayed and played together. We ultimately communicated well beyond the continuous refrains of Buenos Dias.

Our honest effort to share Christ's love with them led to other words that seem much more appropriate. *Hope, dignity, family* and *sacrificial love* seem far more accurate. Yes, life in a batey or poor rural community is extremely difficult, even sometimes impossible, but the people there welcome our love and are open to the lifesaving message of our Lord. Being there opened our hearts in a way that cannot be accomplished by reading or studying. It must instead be experienced.

I was finally ready to step out of my comfort zone and into the mission field in earnest, and the Dominican bateys quickly became a second home.

Life Lesson 4

When the Holy Spirit leads you somewhere in mission, and you are open to the voice of God on your heart, buckle up for a great ride.

From Moises to you:

If we could just provide enough clean water, we would eliminate 90% of disease. The world could then stop its focus on spending billions of dollars in creating new medicines that just treat symptoms instead of the problem.

We try hard to pay forward the blessing we get from Water@Work and other NGO's by providing quality healthcare and compassion to the poorest in our country. We will forever be grateful.

5. Everyone Gets a Mulligan, Right?

"Come, let us build ourselves a city and a tower with its top in the heavens, and let us make a name for ourselves..."

Genesis11:4

After that first trip to the Dominican I was on fire to help; absolutely convinced that God wanted me to bring clean water to the rural poor of the Dominican that needed help so badly. It's impossible to actually describe a calling. God never uttered clear instructions on either a computer or stone tablet. But I walked away with an absolute certainty that I had to help. I came back and shared with my brother Steve my vision, my prayer, my hope, and my conviction to do this. Not surprisingly, he agreed and was all in. You see, Steve and I have an incredible relationship.

Not that it started out so incredible. Steve is two and a half years my elder, has four inches on me in height, and about fifty pounds in weight. The proportions were the same growing up, albeit just smaller. In any event, the two of us grew up very close. Close as measured by the fact that we had one very small bedroom to share, a very small "TV Room", and not much more space. As the sons of Italian immigrants in an ethnic section of Chicago, we were quite literally on top of each other all the time. In the 1960's TV wrestling was a big thing, as were the Three Stooges. As I remember it, and Steve would disagree, the two combined to render me the victim of our brotherly jostling nearly every day.

However, our father was always intent on the two of us staying close. I don't think he could have imagined just how close we have become. The same big brother that pummeled me into submission nearly every day as kids has become the same big brother that I would start and grow a successful water purification business with.

He is the same big brother that I would go into ministry with, and come to rely on for friendship, spiritual healing, business advice, and just about anything one person can depend on from another.

First Water Systems, Inc. is the name of our water company and it has facilitated my exposure to the global realities involved in providing clean water to those in need. After several years of learning just about everything we could on microbiology and working with some really smart folks, we developed a full line of exceptional products. Our primary offerings met virtually all of our customer needs for U.S. based emergency water and provided stable growth.

In a short time, we developed permanently mounted systems that were perfect for villages, schools, clinics and orphanages in international markets. Even though we were soon shipping our systems to all parts of the world, my heart would regularly return me to the Dominican and the people that I both loved and felt I could personally help.

This Feels Good!

Our first non-profit efforts were to simply build purification systems from the profits of our company, and go to the Dominican and install them. We did this several times because, quite frankly, it was easy and simply felt good. How could one not feel incredible knowing that his technology and time in-country were making a tangible difference? There's nothing like holding a baby and knowing that she will be there the next time you visit because her precious life will not be lost to rampant water-borne disease.

Then a strange but wonderful thing happened. Our business got busy. Really busy. We were blessed with the kind of growth that can make a head swim. On the flip side though, our ability to service and continue to visit the Dominican with any regularity was seriously diminishing. Without regular visits the systems we installed needed more and more maintenance and repairs. We began getting an increasing number of calls to go down and change filters, UV bulbs and pumps (so why do all pumps purchased outside the US burn out so quickly?).

As we endeavored to find the time to go and maintain the systems, we began to realize that we were becoming part of the problem. We were unwittingly perpetuating the disabling demon of dependency.

✓ **Gut Check 1**: We were creating a monster that reinforced and amplified the issue of dependency that had so crushed Haiti whereas most of the other people we served had managed to escape it.

The fear that we might not be able to support these installations in the future because our business could not afford it or because we couldn't physically be there to do the work began to override the feel-goods. A potential situation where the people that had gotten used to good clean water would be forced to revert back to disease infested ditch water began. Bodies once used to healthy water and then returned to contaminated water would be in even more ruinous condition than what we had originally found.

✓ **Gut Check 2:** Neither Steve or I, nor our company, could be the solution to the problem despite any level of resources thrown at it.

If all that weren't enough, nothing we were doing helped spread the gospel to these at-risk people. Instead of focusing on God, theirs was on daily survival or the deceptive voodoo that was always close by. Our "spiritual feel-good" was really suffering. While we certainly enjoyed sharing Christ's love with the residents when in-country, a few weeks a year is hardly a good solution for evangelizing a huge at-risk population.

✓ **Gut Check 3:** The blessings we received enabled us to help, yet God was only a very small part of the conversation.

If You Build It, They Will Come

Ultimately, we determined the need to put some constructive structure around our efforts. We decided to stop installing additional systems at even more villages. Changing our focus and creating a non-profit organization promised a mechanism to resolve the three gut check issues that our earlier efforts created. So with healthy doses of enthusiasm and money, we did just that.

We set out to form the kind of organization that would operate in a business-like manner, be there for the long term, and attract other donor organizations. As a retired Vice President at Coca Cola, Steve used his serious connections to bring in some good folks with incredible resumes. Fairly soon, our Board of Directors was complete and seriously qualified. A formal 501 (c) 3 designation followed and, with the addition of some staff, we were ready to jump back into the work we loved so much.

Things progressed rapidly and it began to look like this would be it. We built a solid organization, funded its needs so that everyone could focus on implementing solutions, and looked forward to knocking down those pesky gut checks. Our creation lacked nothing except one critical factor.

But first, let me first explain that Steve and I could not be on the Board of Directors or really have any significant voting rights. As the owners of the for-profit company supplying the water purification systems, we could not have any formal responsibility in the non-profit. Even though we supplied the systems at our cost to make them, we were really officially volunteers to the organization.

At first, we were actually fine with that. We were happy to be the servants while letting others steer the ship. Truly, it was liberating to let others make the decisions while we focused on the nitty-gritty detail of implementing fairly complex technology in a place with little to no resources, and where illiteracy is by far the norm.

Unfortunately, as time went on the ship made some hard turns that didn't quite jibe with our vision. Specifically, God was essentially removed from the equation. Concluding that "the big money" could only be found at large humanitarian organizations and NGOs that would be offended at a reliance and dependence on Christ, the Board took out any mention of God or Christ from all marketing material, documentation and website. We had become an efficient secular organization that was moving in a very different direction than Steve and I felt comfortable with. Our meetings that used to rely on prayer for discernment and direction relied instead on human efforts and personal connections.

All the money and labor we expended couldn't compensate for the lack of Christ in the effort.

It didn't take too long to realize that this serious disconnect could not be resolved. That, plus the personality conflicts that inevitably will rise when there is a core disagreement on an elemental issue like the one we faced, resulted in Steve and I essentially being asked to leave the organization.

Crushed is the only adequate word for how we felt. We had poured immeasurable amounts of time, talent, and treasure into the creation and stabilization of this new organization only to be considered a stranger to it within a couple short years.

Not History, Prologue

We went through all the emotions one would expect to experience with the loss of something so important or special. Ultimately though, for the next two years we simply gave up. We had become victims of our worst fears. Adding even more distress, we erroneously assumed that the organization would support the villages we had previously put systems into. This assumption was also incorrect, as they unfortunately either didn't, or couldn't, cover them all with any regularity. Without critical maintenance visits, many systems fell into disrepair. Over time the people in the villages had become dependent on us and "we" ultimately failed them.

In his masterpiece *The Tempest*, William Shakespeare first uses the expression "What's past is prologue". His reference is that everything that has happened in the past has led the characters to do what they are about to do. In essence, the past fated them to their future. While I don't believe in fate, the more contemporary definition of prologue is that the past merely sets the stage for the next event.

When used in the context of a play, the past simply becomes necessary for a future act, but is actually not overly important to the main story. And that is the rationale that enabled us to dust the sand from our sandals and get back in the game.

One Step Back, Two Steps Forward

The step back we experienced was a big one - a really big one. However, throughout the depression and (honestly) self-pity that we had just gone through, I continued to feel the undeniable call to help the people in the poor rural Dominican villages through the blessing of clean water. There are many stories in the Bible of God's relentless love. He continually chooses and empowers unworthy people that truly just don't get it.

Like Jonah, we can run, but we can't hide. When He chases and won't give up on us, even the most hardened soul ultimately relents. I was at that place where I wanted to give up and go back to the comfortable life that was merely one decision away. People that know me well readily speak about how I aged a decade in those brief couple of years.

Every earthly reason to stop my involvement was on display, and the Evil One had a field day. The embarrassment and shame of having to tell friends and supporters that I had to walk away from the organization I was so passionate about—the very same organization that many of them had supported with their prayers and financial support—was omnipresent.

And yet, thankfully, God would not give up on me and the vision He had placed on my heart.

So putting the shame behind, I did the best I could to document all the good, bad, and ugly that I had experienced since that first mission trip. I was determined to look at what happened as prologue, where it dynamically sets up the future, and not as static history that one tries to forget. There were many lessons to learn, and if I was to try yet again I was determined to learn from the past and not repeat its mistakes. I was also going to take the time to pray earnestly not only for guidance and discernment, but also for forgiveness.

Guilt is an ugly thing and totally against biblical truths. Still, it was hard to overcome the long entangling briar patch that I had dragged my family, bother, friends, co-workers and supporters through. I eventually realized the problems and feelings caused by my good intentions were meant to be the crucible fire that tempered and honed me for what was coming. Through the walls of my human ambitions and many limitations, the Holy Spirit found the cracks to pour into me.

As time moved along a little further and another couple years passed, solutions to our earlier problems became revealed. I was also becoming more energized than ever before, and ready to try it again but with the glorification of God being the first and foremost goal.

Life Lesson 5

Trust the Apostle Paul when he said: "that for those who love God all things work together for good, for those who are called according to his purpose".

From Steve to you:

A small business owner that takes his Christian obligation seriously is no different than any other Christian ... save the fact that a small business person might have greater resources and certainly greater flexibility to share the love of Christ through his actions.

As Christians, we have the obligation to help our Christian brothers and sisters. Whether through donation (money), dedication (time) or devotion (prayer), Christians must embody in their actions what Christ asks from us.

We are blessed at First Water to have a successful business and a product that makes a difference in the lives of so many. But the small business realities we face are not any different than other small businesses. Recognizing how blessed we are in the United Sates ... giving back shouldn't be that hard.

Part 2

The Birth of Something Special

6. Caution, Objects in the Mirror Appear Larger Than They Are...

> *"And after you have suffered a little while, the God of all grace, who has called you to his eternal glory in Christ, will himself restore, confirm, strengthen, and establish you."*
>
> 1 Peter 5:10

It was time to be smart about our passion. We had been through a lot and I was only really sure about one thing. While we had made mistakes, taken wrong turns, and not taken the time to plan for the future like a good business would, I was still confident that God had called me to this specific mission.

Actually, we just couldn't afford any additional structural missteps. First and foremost, that meant the establishment of serious prayer time and acknowledgement in no uncertain terms that God was at the helm. Whereas before we knew that we needed a light to follow, we now realized that not only were we in the dark, but in unfamiliar territory as well. We tried this non-profit thing with all the human strength and capabilities we could, and fell short. From here on out, God would lead and we would patiently work within His time.

It was also time to identify the gifts that we could offer and, more importantly, the areas of weakness where we needed to pray for Him to supply resources. Our gifts, as humble as they were, primarily encompassed our passion, life experiences, and whatever remaining treasure we could scrounge up. You may be familiar with the expression "you only know what you know." As primarily business folks, the one thing we knew was that we needed to put some healthy business principles around our desire to glorify Him.

We needed to develop a Vision Plan.

I have been blessed to start and grow several successful businesses in my past. Each was a learning experience in something I had never studied formally nor could even spell at first: entrepreneurship. As such, growth was achieved through trial and error, gut feelings, and pure energy. All of these are good things of serious value, but at best complimentary to the necessity of having a good plan.

Dov Charney, founder and CEO of American Apparel, a clothing manufacturer, wholesaler, retailer, and true entrepreneurial success story, has said: *"Passion. That's it. When you believe in what you're doing, that's it."* Henry Ford, an icon of American business and founder of Ford Motor Company once said: *"You can do anything if you have enthusiasm."*

I fully agree with both of these hugely successful people, in that passion and enthusiasm are critical and can overcome many obstacles. Particularly in non-profits, passion can inspire others like nothing else and is highly contagious.

You can out-distance that which is running after you, but not what is running inside you.
— Rwandan Proverb

However, I have also seen many ministries that rely almost solely on passion and never successfully progress on to the next critical steps. They inevitably lament and wonder why the rest of the world doesn't share in their particular passion. The question in their minds, and oftentimes on their lips, is "How can they not understand how (insert any particularly worthy cause) is so critical? Why are they not as excited as I am?" True success ultimately takes much more than just passion. It takes careful and determined planning, and actions that lie within the will of our heavenly father.

We Need More Wall Space!

Up to this point we have met many great people that set the stage for the realization of the vision. From here on out, though, we will be introduced to incredible people of God that have had an incalculable impact on the birthing, growth, and operation of our ministry, Water@Work.

It is truly difficult to not write chapters on each person. Their critical thinking and often herculean efforts have brought us to where we are. Because it would start to sound unbelievable after a while, we will focus on just a dozen or so individuals that represent the many. Please know that every person we meet from here on was sent directly from God and can never be thanked enough. So for starters, let's meet Tim Fenbert, the first of these angels.

Tim is a financial guru that helps business people make wise choices concerning investments and wealth management. He is also an Elder in the Presbyterian Church, a very active husband and dad, and a very spiritual person. Tim is one of those rare sorts that can navigate the waters of practiced discipleship atop the stormy seas and still see a bright horizon; he's the kind of person you have a great time with whether praying or watching a sporting event.

While discussing business over lunch one day, I started talking about my desire that my for-profit business could somehow support my non-profit ministry dream. I shared with him the years of frustration and failure, as well as my still persistent calling. His immediate response of "Maybe I can help?" wasn't exactly a surprise, but certainly encouraged me. We agreed that the best way to proceed would be through a Retreat. It would be a wonderful opportunity to pull back to a quiet place without distractions where we could begin to organize and plan.

In reading the gospels, one cannot miss the number of times Christ pulled away from the crowds and distractions to have a "retreat" with His heavenly father. Those focused times of prayer solidified his commitment, provided clear direction, and led to purposeful actions that followed God's will. Sounds exactly like what we needed!

We at Water@Work retreat regularly. It seems that we can never have too much time in focused effort to discern where we should go and the best way to get there. If you or your organization is not in the habit of utilizing this tremendous tool, I would strongly encourage it for virtually any issue you may be dealing with.

At our first retreat, Tim and I were tempted to immediately jump into the hopes, dreams, and vision of Water@Work. Instead, however, we documented all the early failings and lessons learned. This was particularly painful, but entirely enlightening. Tim's fresh look at the events of the past brought a new perspective. We rifled through the large easel pad paper so quickly that we ran out of wall space to stick them to. For every identified failure, we countered with a correcting method. Every circuitous route was straightened.

The effort became the beginning of our Vision Plan. While a Vision Plan can be fairly foreign to non-profits, it is considered essential to successful for-profit businesses in high growth enterprises. It is a highly valuable tool that identifies everything from Mission Statements and Vision Statements to growth expectations and budgets. It forces the *advance* thinking of what the mission will strive to be and do, and then documents the steps required to achieve the mission. It is however far more than just a road map. It recognizes not just lessons learned but best practices as well. The past truly becomes prologue and not history. It represents the embodiment of the dream and sets expectations for organized, pragmatic growth.

A common reason for not developing a plan is the fear of not having the perfect plan. However, it is important to realize that any effort in this area will be added to, corrected, expanded, and dissected many times on the path towards an eventually successful working plan. As General George S. Patton once famously said about his penchant for decisive decision making:

> *"A good plan executed now is better than a perfect plan executed next week."*

The exercise and our subsequent efforts led to a model for moving forward that was unlike anything we had seen anywhere else. The painful and discouraging past was lending itself to a great new jumping forward point. Its issues were seen as objects in a rear view mirror and relegated to memory. Their toxic nature no longer choked us and we could put them into perspective. The next step was to now put ourselves in the future and perform a backward analysis that would ensure long term success.

A Backward Look at Success

Oftentimes, entrepreneurs either can't see far enough into the future or don't have a big enough goal to facilitate them starting at the end. After all, there's a good reason the old Chinese saying of "Failing to plan is planning to fail" has been around for millennia. It is a common error that can stymie any effort early on and result in disappointment. I certainly have been guilty of this malady.

Fortunately, Tim's extensive involvement with small business owners gave him a critical perspective that made all the difference. Drawing from our experiences in this regard, we looked at many critical ministry functions and viewed them from the desired outcome backward. We identified a preferred result and worked backwards in a fairly exhaustive manner. Throughout the remainder of this book, we will come back and discuss how this business tenet has led to much ministry success over the years.

Defining what success should embody may appear like an easy and obvious exercise, and it perhaps is in some areas. But going through it ensures that all processes are accounted for and, most importantly, that the customer or reason for service is always the most important thing. Customer-centric thinking is extremely important in developing the processes that will lead to an exceptional delivery of services.

Basically, the question becomes *"What do we want to be and look like when we grow up?"* Or, stated more maturely, *"What does success ultimately appear like?"* This simple first step is a critical one. In our case, we started with three major pillars of the organization that would drive everything else. We called them our Three Big Drops. These focused on what is referred to as "forward think" and, if properly implemented, would yield success. Our Three Big Drops were:

1. **Improve Health** - Access to clean water eliminates water-related disease, the most common cause of illness and death in the world and, more precisely, the Dominican Republic where we sought to serve. By dramatically improving health, clean water will also increase resident income, reduce medical expenses, and increase school attendance.

   Goal One is the provision of good health through clean water to every person living in the poor rural Dominican communities and bateys.

2. **Create Economic Stability** - Partner with local churches in the communities to help them sell the clean water to local families at a price affordable to everyone. If there are some that completely lack the resources to pay for the clean water, empower the local pastor to selectively provide it free of charge. All the monies earned from the water sales should stay in-country for the benefit of the community. They should first be used to maintain the purification equipment and, secondarily, to pay for much-needed community development projects such as building schools, latrines, and community gardens.

   Goal Two is the establishment of self-sustainability and genuine commerce in communities that have little to none, as well as a mechanism for community development that is entirely local.

3. **Access to the Gospel** – By going to church to get their clean water, residents will also hear about the "living water" of Jesus Christ. The tie between clean water and living water is a natural way to introduce the gospel message. Utilizing the local churches and Christ-based organizations to deliver the clean water also improves their stature and relevance in the community. Residents appreciate the church providing its most basic need that nobody else has done or will do.

Goal Three *is the growth of the local church, and for every resident to know and embrace Jesus Christ as their Lord and Savior.*

Clearly articulated and understood forward-looking goals are paramount to guiding any organization ahead. They tend to be the embodiment of the vision and the mark against which every strategic decision is measured. For us the Three Big Drops were also used to very succinctly tell our story.

In addition to these forward thinking doctrines, we also identified what we wanted to avoid in the ministry. These can be thought of as forewarning goals that keep organizations on the correct path or "backward think." Key aspects we set in place included:

1. **An effort of the Body of Christ** – success needs to be viewed as the power of the Holy Spirit working through the body of Christ, and not by any individual organization or government.

2. **Focus on core competencies** – we must avoid *mission creep* and just endeavor to do one thing right in one place.

3. **Rely on human compliance metrics** – we will monitor how well we execute at every step, and quickly implement improvements when warranted.

4. **Rely on Godly compliance metrics** – we will trust in God to be responsible for success and growth, and watch for any movement outside His will.

5. **Avoid a cult of personality** – no individual should become so important that the organization is measured or known by that individual.

Dodging Bullets

A strange thing happened as we completed our Vision Plan for the new non-profit venture. Things at work got very crazy for both

Tim and myself and we encountered significant personal issues. Both Tim's family and mine went through some extremely trying times. It was all we could do to get together on a very infrequent basis. To use a common football analogy, we weren't fumbling the ball, but every yard was a thorough struggle and the goal line seemed a long way off.

There's an old Air Force saying that says you can be certain you are flying close to or over a target when the enemy steps up its resistance and the incoming fire gets closer and more frequent. We surely felt our spiritual enemy firing at us. It doesn't take much research to realize that this is a fairly common occurrence. You can be assured that as you get involved in ministry while still attempting to succeed in your "day gig", the Evil One will do his best to derail your efforts. Worse yet, he attacks where we are the most vulnerable, including the ones you love and protect, a stable income, good health, important career developments, and so on.

Thankfully, when our ministry efforts are grounded in serving Christ and anointed by God, we stand assured by Romans 8:28. *"We know that all things work together for good for those who love God, who are called according to his purpose."*

Tim and I became unwitting examples of the difficulty in doing missions while trying to manage the daily expectations of family and career. I pray that you can persevere as the world throws every sort of difficulty in your path towards Christian service. Many that have been significantly challenged by the fallen world will tell you that it was service work that got them through it. When we spend time working in ministry, we generally serve folks in significant need or trouble. The ministry that focuses on serving healthy, successful believers in Christ that are devoid of any issues simply doesn't exist. Rather, a focus on others and their struggles tends to minimize the time and energy spent on our own troubles. In our case, we get to serve the ultra-poor that lack access to the Gospel, clean water, or a future.

Tim would agree that one's personal issues always pale in comparison. Quite frankly, it's often impossible to even remember what has been troubling me while I am focused upon and in service to these dear brothers and sisters. This must be true because through it all, Tim's involvement has actually expanded and gotten much deeper. He has served in many capacities and has even gone on to become the organization's President of the Board of Directors.

In any event, through the trials of our times, we were able to document the critical items that had derailed the earlier efforts, and begin to formulate and implement mechanisms to overcome them.

We had a first cut at a Plan, and prayerfully moved along.

Life Lesson 6
The key to all success is threefold:

1. Seek Godly guidance and direction,
2. Act boldly,
3. Enjoy watching God do His thing.

From Tim to you:

I have certainly been on a roller coaster in my life on many levels. There were even times I had no idea how things could possibly work out. I ended up realizing the only lifeboat in the sea was the God I continually turned to. When Tom and I first started discussing Water@Work, I never dreamed it would become the impactful organization it has. And I never thought I would become so involved!

Since those humble first beginnings, I have traveled to the Dominican on many occasions, served as the organization book keeper, Steering Committee Leader, Prayer Advocate and, most recently, the Chairman of the Board of Directors. It has truly been a labor of love. Love for the people we serve, love for our team, and love for the incredible God that makes it all happen.

This is how I got through the most difficult times of my life--service to those that are in truly dire need, for the glory of God. I would suggest it to anyone. It beats pulling your hair out and constantly worrying.

7. Water@Work Breathes at Last

*"In the beginning God created the heavens
and the earth ... and the Spirit of God was
hovering over the face of the waters."*

Genesis 1:1-2

Starting anything of value takes significant amounts of time and commitment. Even God took six heavenly days! Being involved in an early stage ministry is no different. There are lots of things to do and never enough time, but it can be exceptionally rewarding.

The reverse is also true in that there are many people that enjoy and are inspired by established ministries and non-profits. They are either drawn to the great work they are doing, the terrific people that serve through it, or the safety that comes from having weathered the challenges of organizational formation. Things are running fairly smoothly and it is easy for them to envision a good fit. Their particular talents can be strategically utilized and easily integrated into existing operations, and they feel led to help grow or sustain that particular mission. In the mature organization, one's initial effort is primarily fitting in with the team that one works with, and understanding the mission and your place in it.

If you have the entrepreneurial bent like Tim and I, then you may feel more comfortable starting something new or getting involved at an early stage. There are many early stage missions that typically have minimal staff or other people that are actively involved. In these types of organizations, one's talents could really be critical to sustaining success. Here there is more risk and personal exposure, but the rewards are commensurately fulfilling. You might be asked to be involved with anything from coordinating volunteers to becoming the Executive Director.

Being small and nimble facilitates creativity. Without the inertia of "well, we've just always done it this way," creative new solutions can be administered to old problems. Among the positive take-aways are the opportunities for active engagement, to fully follow God's direction even if it is contrarian to conventional thinking, and to try different approaches.

Early stage or start-up missions demand significant initial effort. There are a tremendous amount of details that need to be tackled to simply get rolling. Water@Work was no exception. Actually, the level of effort was significantly greater because it is an international ministry. As such, not only do you have the normal issues and challenges of start-up and growth, but international ministries have the additional burden of a foreign language, culture, and governmental challenges.

If we were going to be successful, it was going to take God's active leadership and a good number of angels with specific talents.

Casting the Net

Tim and I had made a hearty effort at an initial model for Water@Work. We even chose the name because it helped tell our story. We don't view the delivery of water as the end game. Water@Work is in the business of introducing souls to Christ, expanding the church, and building healthy bodies and strong communities.

Water is simply the vehicle that facilitates that. The water *is at work* to achieve the goals God placed on our hearts. It became pretty clear early on however that we were going to need a commensurately God-sized amount of assistance and expertise.

We prayed diligently for God to send the specific people required to see His mission through. We also started talking to everyone we knew about the start-up ministry and our needs...and I do mean everyone. You never know where or when God will supply an angel, but if you aren't out there being a nuisance and continually looking for opportunities, there's a good chance the perfect person may slip through the net. It's okay to be persistent. It is something akin to evangelism. In a polite and correct way, one should always be planting seeds. If the recipient of the message is intrigued or accepting, then give it to them good!

A friend of a business associate introduced us to Robbie Gring Campbell, a very accomplished marketing professional who had great connections into the world of marketing and communications. This was a total answer to prayer. While we had a water technology solution, we needed assistance in getting the story out. Very quickly, Robbie blessed us with Kevin, who made his living designing websites, and David, a branding and graphics professional.

Robbie is a special person that has one of the biggest hearts for God that I have ever met. She has weathered incredible trials in her recent life and continues to completely trust God in every way. Like many, her business essentially flat-lined during the Great Recession. Even while dealing with that huge hit and a staggering material loss even greater than most endured, she still attended every meeting. She also managed to brighten the room when she was around, and served part time as our initial Executive Director.

It would be reasonable to think that Water@Work might have suffered during the Great Recession. I mean, what would the odds of success be for starting a new international ministry during the worst economic climate in nearly one hundred years?

During this early time, every person involved in the ministry suffered great personal setbacks in different ways. No one was exempt. Yet each time, God saw us through and our little group of dreamers held each other up. Every one of our meetings, not just then but now as well, begins with a time of worship and prayer. And when the business meeting concludes, we end with prayer requests and praises. Everyone involved became very close and are freely open with each other regarding our personal struggles and joys. During the first two or so years of Water@Work, there were definitely more prayer requests than praises. God most assuredly knit us together.

When God knows the purpose of your service is to honor Him, He will honor your faith and provide for all your daily needs.

We would often laugh at how God had put together this group of "nobodies" for this incredibly important work. Irrepressibly no matter how bad things got for us individually, the ministry kept moving forward. Even though we lacked a celebrity or significant "connection" in the community, we operated on the assumption that God was at the lead and we just kept putting one foot in front of the other. Because we believed that what we were doing was so important, we weren't going to let anything keep us down.

We were also committed to volunteer service. Aside from an individual receiving a small stipend here or there, all the money we received was to go to the people we served in the Dominican. This is hard to achieve. It was and still is really difficult to maintain fiscal discipline in light of the huge needs our teammates faced. However, one of the hard lessons learned previously was to get people involved because their hearts were in it and not because there were dollars in it. In the previous organization, we had put nice salaries in place for key people and the result was an organization not driven by the principles we cherished.

We serve to love and honor God, and trust he will provide our daily bread. Even today, with many full time and committed individuals, Water@Work maintains a very minimum salary burden.

Once Kevin created the first iteration of our website, we began to feel we really had something. While it was limited in functionality, the very act of creating a live site where others can go to see one's vision is tremendous. Every small move forward like this becomes a giant leap and confirms that you are on the right track.

Creating a Product

There are many different thoughts on the paradigms that non-profits operate under. Some are so creative, particularly in social media, that they make for-profit businesses green with envy. Many others are unfortunately plagued by bureaucracy and sloth-like movement. After serving as both a volunteer and on the Boards of Directors of both small and large non-profits, I certainly have my own perspective. However, we will avoid that particular rant and instead focus on the attempt by Water@Work to integrate sound business practices into its non-profit environment.

Part of that business perspective is the understanding that we have multiple customers to serve, again starting at the finish and working backwards to establish the order of importance:

- Most Important: the batey or Dominican resident that purchases a jug of water
- Second Most Important: the pastor at the local church who is blessed with one of the Water@Work water plants
- Third Most Important: the donor that provides the money to build the water plant

All of these "customers" deserve a superior product. This means:

- In the case of the batey resident, he needs clean, healthy water delivered at a price he can afford.
- The pastor needs a business model that is adapted to his and the community's realities and educational level.
- The donor needs a well stewarded organization and a coherent message that is both compelling and matches her reasons for giving.

Building a Value Proposition

Having a great product is paramount, but unless the prospective customer clearly sees its value, it will likely fail. Once value is defined for all customer groups, the model for implementing it to all parties can be structured.

Value in any enterprise can be difficult to model. Defining value within a customer group may not be overly challenging, but modeling procedures and practices that reinforce or measure value can indeed be very problematic.

As a potential donor of time or money you may have experienced this. Have you ever considered giving to a mission only to find that they couldn't provide any metrics on success, or adequately define exactly how they would use your gift, or clearly show impact from their efforts? It is frustrating and ultimately turns many away from fruitful service or the blessing of giving. Professionalism in the delivery of services and processes ranks right up there with passion in attracting people.

While your specific consideration is likely different than others, every person that contributes has some criteria that they use to verify value before giving their time, treasure, or talent. Water@Work has been rightfully questioned many times concerning value within its paradigm, confronted with questions such as:

- How many baptisms or new church members are there as a result of a water plant being donated?
- How clean is the water compared to US standards, and is there verifying tests?
- Does the government recognize and support your efforts?
- How much profit can a local church that receives a water plant expect annually?
- How is sustainability for the future guaranteed?
- How will my talents or gifts make a concrete difference?

While difficult to measure at times, the value proposition is important to everyone involved from the development of the product to its implementation, and needs to be constantly challenged. Every new process or procedure must always either reinforce or improve the value proposition to the organization's customers.

Creating a Brand

One of the development tasks that Robbie encouraged us to undergo was the creation and enforcement of a brand identity. Her insistence on a developing a memorable brand has certainly been valuable both in-country and here in America. Branding can be incredibly powerful and can help in product or identity development and customer retention.

A successful brand is easily recognized and brings about a positive feeling when thought of. An excellent example is Coca-Cola. There are few places on earth where the Coca-Cola brand is not immediately recognized. As Interbrand, a premier rating service of business brands, has written:

> *"Guided by its 2020 Vision goals around innovation, focus, and creativity, Coca-Cola achieves impressive global presence through standout ad campaigns, bold design, digital savvy, and a simple, universally relevant theme that weaves throughout the brand's communications: happiness."*

Creating and encouraging happiness is constantly used in every communication. Coupling that with their easily recognizable logo is the key concept within the Coca-Cola brand.

Water@Work, through the leadership and diligent work of Robbie and David, birthed a very identifiable logo that is used in all communications and is painted on every water plant in the Dominican. The logo is seen, recognized, and adding value to all three of our customer groups by identifying a consistent, quality product that a customer can trust. Our prayer is that the central word thought of with our brand would be quality; quality product, water, people, and accountability.

A brand association word like "happiness" or "quality" is difficult and took time to evolve within Water@Work. Summing up the essence of the organization that would resonate with all three customer groups was initially challenging. However after many iterations God placed an expression on our hearts that we all absolutely loved:

> *"Dirty water to clean water - clean water to living water"*

It is what we do, what we feel, and what we measure ourselves against. It is also clearly understood by all our customers and is language-neutral.

We had come a long way, but it would take some serious organizational growth to achieve the significance we sought.

Life Lesson 7
Just start the ball rolling. God will provide the occasional course corrections as necessary.

From Robbie to you:

The telling of our personal stories through the discovery of the magnitude and love of The Almighty is how we share our experiences of God in our lives.

I have come to understand that our real purpose in life is to help others experience their own personal relationship with God. Yet, until my "yes" to God for sacrificing more than I ever dreamed I might to Water@Work Ministry, I had little to no knowledge of what it meant to help others experience their own relationship with God. I was more focused on my experience than on helping others with their experiences.

Life before Water@Work was all about me ... building a career and a national reputation for my expertise. Traveling anywhere, I desired and used resources without involving God's desires for my life. Yet, the Living God used the formation and infancy of this 501c3 entity to "break me, melt me, mold me and fill me" beyond what I might consider possible.

Making a commitment to the Water@Work ministry changed my life forever and caused me to STOP and consider the importance of a true Christian "testimony" regarding God's work in my life.

8. Organizational Development at Home

"If the whole body were an eye, where would the sense of hearing be? If the whole body were an ear, where would the sense of smell be? But in fact God has placed the parts in the body, every one of them, just as he wanted them to be. If they were all one part, where would the body be? As it is, there are many parts, but one body."

1 Corinthians 12:17-20

God certainly heard our prayers and poured forth many wonderful people with skill sets and talents that seemed custom fit. On one occasion I was introduced to the prolific author and retired Presbyterian pastor, Cecil Murphy. An early goal of mine was to record everything that could one day serve as a learning aid to future missional entrepreneurs. We had hoped that he would join us and document all the tribulations and joys of our adventure. Unfortunately he couldn't devote the time, but he suggested a person that might be able to help.

That person was Patrick Borders, and he is indeed a rare breed. He has a similar background as me, but is completely different in just about every way possible – personality type, management style, demeanor, communication style – and I absolutely love him. He similarly started his professional life out as an engineer, but moved into sales and then writing. He possesses a unique ability to think and problem-solve like an engineer, yet he communicates with a confident humility. He was able to understand the technical nuances, capabilities and limitations of the water purification solution we were developing, yet master creative challenges like organizational structuring and communications.

In a theme that we shall see repeat, God crossed our paths at a uniquely perfect time. Patrick wasn't fulfilled by the job he had. He was living an unassuming suburban life with two great kids and a wonderful wife that taught at the local elementary school. But like many of us he felt he was living short of his potential. Nothing in particular was wrong; he just knew he could be much more.

Patrick started praying specifically for enlightenment on his future. Then as he continued his daily conversations with God, he lost his father. This terrible event brought him to the edge and caused a thorough review of where he was and, more importantly where he was going.

Over lunch I spoke with Patrick and we shared many personal things. We comforted each other and prayed together. Some tears were shed and wounds made better. Towards the end of our time together, I brought up the ministry dream I had. It wasn't a carefully crafted presentation of our budding organization, but rather an idea and commitment to serve Christ. In a way that only God can do, He used that last 10% of our conversation to stir Patrick's heart. Shortly thereafter we got together again and on this occasion 90% of the time shifted to discussing Water@Work.

Patrick began volunteering as our principal communicator. He wrote blogs, website content and press releases. His natural writing abilities coupled with his increasing knowledge of our mission led to a much more professional outward communication. He was gaining an intellectual connection, but desired more. As soon as was practical, he accompanied me down for his first trip in-country. I should also note that Patrick is not shy about reminding me that at this point he has more Dominican passport stamps than I do!

We have found that the organization is best served when critical people start with limited activities and then grow into a greater role after fully grasping everything that the ministry embodies.

In typical fashion of all those that visit the mission field, Patrick quickly fell in love with the local people we wanted to serve. I do not write that casually. We serve there because we truly love these people, dirt and all. It usually starts with the children and grows from there. We envision each child as our own and every community as if we lived there. The personal connections are where the all-important passion comes from. Patrick was caught in God's great ministry net and he was excited to have his prayers answered.

We had gotten pretty far with a very part time Executive Director, and knew we couldn't go much further without a greater commitment. If you are not familiar with the role of an Executive Director, picture a CEO, senior manager, staff member and bottle washer, perhaps with a little head coach and lion tamer, all rolled into one person. Patrick offered to step in as a volunteer as long as he could continue earning his living writing. While not the most perfect resume for an Executive Director, his genuine commitment to Christ and our customers made him seem like a natural fit. He received his call and was perfect for us!

We have experienced during our early-stage phase that the best people to have involved are called by God, and may not have the earthly resume one would expect. Over time, as enough people are involved to fill most organization chart boxes, it is easier to pray for specific talents and wait for God to bring them. Within a year of assuming his limited role, Patrick totally weaned himself from his writing career and blessed us by becoming our full time Executive Director.

Developing a Professional, Christian Culture

A significant drawback to a "shoe-string operation," or one that heavily utilizes volunteers and part time staff, is the lack of organizational culture. As the American industrialist and noted philanthropist Andrew Carnegie once said:

> *"Teamwork is the ability to work together toward a common vision. The ability to direct individual accomplishments*

toward organizational objectives. It is the fuel that allows common people to attain uncommon results".

Achieving this is perhaps hardest of all for an organization like ours. Individuals are often on their own to make decisions and resolve issues. A central body to check and manage effort is simply a luxury that early-stage non-profits cannot afford. As such, it can be very difficult to create and maintain a sense of culture. Meeting monthly or bi-monthly does not necessarily promote the healthy "working together" required to "attain uncommon results" or in some instances, the "common vision" spoken of by Mr. Carnegie.

There were, however, two areas we excelled in. The first was professionalism. While not everyone had professional degrees or credentials (remember we were a group of nobodies!), everyone worked together and supported each other. When one stumbled or required help, two were there to support and lift that individual up. The level of respect among teammates was among the finest I have ever witnessed. Everyone truly respected each other. Perhaps because we were all primarily volunteers, we gave each other a wide berth and generally assumed the best when confused.

The second area where we excelled was in our Christian commitment. We never had a litmus test for working with the ministry such as a particular faith or, as can be more common, anyone but a particular faith. We did however require that only professing Christians need apply. We were all in it to serve our Lord and no matter how good a resume might look or how qualified a person was, we refused to water down (bad pun intended) the central reason we existed.

May the roof above us never fall in; and may the friends gathered below it never fall out.

- Irish Blessing

That's not to say we weren't without our disagreements. To the contrary, people with strong religious, spiritual, and ethical convictions can sometimes find it hard to accept differing thoughts in some areas. While coming to agreement on conflicts is a continuing challenge, it has made each of us better. We set some ground rules and honestly listened when, for example, a more conservative Christian might differ with a less conservative Christian. Acceptable issue resolution generally comes through mutual respect and knowing that the only reason an individual is involved is to serve God the best way they know how.

Still, developing a culture amid the realities we worked in was not exactly easy. Peter Brookshaw, the renowned organizational culturist has addressed the real essence of creating a positive Christian culture:

> *"From a Christian perspective, an organization intent on honoring God will have the blessing of God. I have seen, read and heard of organizations, that have come against great odds, not simply because of the tenacity of the leader or manager, the focus of the team, or 'good luck', but rather the empowerment from God. I firmly believe that organizations that remain focused on God, amongst the whirlwind of organizational life, will have the blessing of God".*

There it is! The key to a successful culture did not lie in our time together, or where we met, or any other earthly characteristic. We would be successful in our desire for organizational culture as long as our focus of service to God remained steadfast. This has rung true throughout our existence. Even during times when we don't meet for many weeks or more, we are confident in our culture through the watchful eye of the Almighty.

One obtains comfort from associating with people of the same ilk, but achieves growth through working with people of differing mindsets.

With Patrick as our leader, we kept this first and foremost. I will never forget the first time Patrick surprised us by administering communion at our Steering Committee meeting. I certainly understand that some faith organizations have strict rules on administering communion and may object, but we thought it a fitting spiritual sacrifice of a group truly focused on Christ. We relied on 1 Peter 2:5 which says: *"Every Christian is considered to be a priest. You also, as living stones, are being built up a spiritual house, a holy priesthood, to offer up spiritual sacrifices acceptable to God through Jesus Christ."*

Ever since then, we typically start formal meetings with the grounding tradition of a devotional and communion.

Oh, There's the Missing Puzzle Piece!

A healthy organization develops in a planned way. We regularly developed and modified our organization chart. The boring "org chart" will certainly never inspire much more than yawns, but it is arguably a very critical step to planning and knowing what to pray for.

Importantly, an org chart should not reflect one's current condition, as is frequently the case, but rather where one wants the organization to go. It should reflect the perfect situation: a graphic representation of the missing pieces that will take your organization towards its vision and goals.

I will also offer that in its development, one should not start at the top as is customary, but rather start at the lowest level utilizing backward think. As we noted earlier, our most important customer requires good clean water in the Dominican (local resident), our next most important customer requires a building, technology, and education (local pastor or Christian community leader), and our next most important customer requires accountability (U.S. churches, donors and organizations).

Recognizing these, we asked ourselves what the best model to meet these customer requirements would look like. As an example, our in-country support team needed people to satisfy the needs of all three customer types. The team would need to fulfill questions such as: *"Will the Water@Work crew or a visiting mission team build the water plant?"* or *"Who will source and secure the materials needed?"* One question leads to another as one works up the org chart and customer type in a chain that results in questions like: *"Who will help market the water and plan for community improvements?"* and *"Who will devise the most effective evangelism program for that particular community?"*

Each of these "who" questions speaks to different customers within the same project and illuminates the type and number of people to satisfy the need. Essentially every bottom-up question must be answered by some box on the org chart. When built this way, from the back to front or bottom to top, the org chart is an indispensable tool in managing people resources. Done properly, the need for committees or sub-committees starts to become clear. Lastly, when God sends an angel wanting to help, you can clearly communicate the areas in need for such a person and their skills.

Careful! You Might Break It

When my son was very young we would play with building blocks for hours on end. He never seemed to get tired of building a new machine, fortress, or alien spacecraft (yes, he has since become an engineer). But the thing he liked more than *building* some imaginative thing, was *breaking* the thing. He would look with pride upon his creation and, after a short time, would gleefully break it all apart. He would then immediately start rebuilding it to make something he thought was an improvement. How liberating!

While I don't advocate breaking organizations apart just to rebuild them, there is great value in looking this way at the organization itself and its service delivery model. Early-stage organizations require this to develop the final model that meets their objectives. Water@Work took many years to achieve its "final" model. While some challenges require minor shifts in delivery, others may resemble seismic shifts that can totally derail the effort. We have experienced both.

With our United States based organization moving ahead well, our focus turned to the critical task of building an in-country team.

Life Lesson 8

There can't be enough planning and modeling done internally *before* significant monies and efforts are expended outwardly.

From Patrick to you:

In my life, I had never once thought that I would someday be the Executive Director of a non-profit ministry. But God is infinitely more creative than we are, and that applies to our vocations as much as anything. Working for Water@Work has been the most fulfilling part of my professional life by far, and I'm grateful for God's direction and provision.

I would encourage everyone to abandon control over their careers and submit themselves to God instead. Only He has the ability to place us where we are most effective and most fulfilled.

9. Organizational Development in the DR

> *"The LORD answered me: Write down this*
> *vision; clearly inscribe it on tablets so one may*
> *easily read it."*
>
> *Habakkuk 2:2*

God has always had a vision for everything—a vision for his creation, a vision for His chosen people, and a vision for you personally. But could it be that the Dominican Republic slipped past His heavenly view? This is an absurd notion of course, but it has at times crossed the minds of many of us involved. Creating an organization in this particular part of the chaotic developing world, and then growing it to meet the incredible expectations of many different people and organizations in both the Dominican and the United States, seemed impossible.

Creating and nurturing our vision for an incredibly low-cost in-country support organization comprised, managed, and financed by Dominicans and Haitians from an organizational perspective should be the very definition of the word "frustration." And yet that was a singularly critical requirement necessary to make Water@Work successful.

Every component of a problem's solution has an important role in the overall and long term successful resolution of that problem. However, in this particular situation it went far beyond important and rose quickly to the *most* important. From our initial discussions on, the goal of developing a strong and independent in-country team that would ensure sustainability long into the future never left our minds and prayers. After all, an argument could be made that it was the core essence of our model.

Unfortunately, the developing world is littered with water purification systems that have long since been abandoned and covered in vines. This is true for both village-wide solutions and those that were intended for individuals or families.

With no long term support structure available, filters go unchanged, membranes get clogged, pumps burn out, people bypass or forget the correct use and maintenance of home based filters, etc. Every technology, or rather the adaptation and delivery mechanism for that technology, will eventually stop working or require maintenance. Reliance on people or resources from America or other foreign sources coming to the rescue is not a viable long term solution. Most of the abandoned technologies one encounters were deployed by well-meaning non-profits that either chose, or had to, move on to other places and problems.

The sad fact is that a change in donors or donation amounts makes a generational commitment impossible. Looking back to one of the original driving forces in the development of Water@Work, we see this very issue. After having originally installed about a half dozen water purification systems at bateys, it became obvious we couldn't support them from America. Money and personnel time were the culprits in our early situation, and are almost always the reason everywhere.

Furthering the situation is the powerful instinctive force of wanting to obtain immediate gratification and satisfaction from one's donations. Not many donors want to see their donation monies spent on an organizational structure located in a faraway place. Funding operations, including buildings, salaries, vehicles, gasoline expenses, testing labs, and so much more isn't very satisfying at a core level. Instead, nearly all donors want to experience that special joy that comes from turning on a working system and seeing the community change.

The picture of smiling healthy children playing in and drinking clean water is, after all, called the "money shot" for a reason. Donations for the mundane support of these systems, especially after many years, nearly always dry up.

Richard Levick, a contributing editor for *Forbes Magazine*, has researched the reality of why non-profit organizations rarely seek funding for operations. I could not agree more with his conclusion:

> *The most respected players in the charity game reinforce the idea that overhead is negative and intrusive, not really part of the business of charity because charity never was or will be a business ... Here's a better idea. Why not reward the charities that have the strongest growth strategies, not just the worthiest social causes.*

The Water@Work growth strategy is built around the idea of community self-support, with a strong in-country presence to reinforce professional development and accountability. No matter what might happen in the future or how many water plants we would build, we needed to ensure that the communities that were blessed with clean water would never have to go back to a state of unclean water.

The first step of the solution was a financial model that guaranteed money would be available from in-country sources. In our case, that meant the sale of water to the community and surrounding environs. The second step however was the people and equipment to make sure that the available money was properly spent on a responsive and capable support organization.

Hey, I Got a Guy ...

When confronted with a significant bump in the road, we have a simple plan: rely on God to provide the answer. After all, if this is truly His ministry; He already has the solution ready at heavenly hand. So after much prayer on this specific issue, we waited for God to identify the person He wanted to spearhead this effort. Given the growing number of water plants that were being funded, we also requested of God to, *ahem*, please respond quickly.

Thankfully He did, and after a short time I was reminded of John Bearden. John is a person that I had met years before at a dinner who felt called to be a United Methodist Volunteer in Mission in the Dominican. When we met, he was struggling with the final go/no decision for uprooting his life and starting over in the Dominican Republic. He had a great and satisfying career in the Georgia Department of Natural Resources with wildlife management, a loving wife, and two small girls between ten and sixteen. I distinctly remember talking about it with my wife and concluding he didn't stand a chance.

> *Leadership in the developing world is really all about loving the people one serves, and then assisting them in growth and relying on them to demonstrate Christian responsibility to lead their society into better times. We shouldn't "do" anything but facilitate and educate.*

Wouldn't it be great if we could receive some sort of points for all the times we get it wrong?

Soon after our dinner, John did indeed move the entire crew down to the Dominican and trusted God to provide the direction for his new life. Fast forward a few years and he was not only an integral support mechanism to local missionaries in the country, but he was also a critical support person in the Evangelical Church of the Dominican Republic, the largest protestant denomination in the country. John became our first In-Country Coordinator, and he made an exceptional leader for our fledgling organizational efforts.

Forget Resumes

John is a strong leader that has blessed many with his mentorship. We aren't talking about a monthly meeting or meal with a young person to see how they are doing. Rather, as John and Donna got to know young local men that they thought could grow into leaders for their country, they took them into their home and mentored them on a daily basis. John passed on his strong work ethic and sense of responsibility, while Donna nurtured them in the ways of family and relationships. Because it is simply part of who they are, they both imparted the vital need for Christ in their lives and continuously modeled what it means to be a disciple of Christ.

After finishing whatever schooling they could afford, the opportunities for employment by young local men in the Dominican are pretty meager. This is particularly true if the person is of Haitian decent or lives in a batey. Both John and Donna felt a responsibility to touch the lives of as many of these souls as possible. They would learn the skills and talents of each by, literally, living with them. Every waking minute was spent with one or more of these men. They prayed together, ate together, learned each other's languages together, experienced life together, and became surrogate parents to many.

In the process, they honed or expanded each protégé's skills so they could make a contribution and get gainful employment. John once said that his funniest memories of his time there was watching the guys laughing and picking at each other like young friends do, while he didn't have a clue as to what was going on.

However, John had a decision to make that would be one of the hardest in his life. He needed to come back to America and work another five years for the state of Georgia so that he could receive a pension and provide for their retirement. John would tell you that this was the hardest decision he faced since the one that originally sent him to the Dominican Republic. But it was also a great test to determine the effectiveness of the model. Could local Dominicans and Haitians, after proper mentoring and training, be relied on to take over the in-country support organization?

This was no easy task, and today John misses the young men he mentored every hour of every day. But it has also been a huge blessing to see over time how the young men did indeed take over and successfully provide critical technical, construction and spiritual support. At the time everyone at Water@Work feared for our in-country operations as a result of John coming back.

John and I were probably the worst. We just didn't want to let go. For all the talk and planning, one would think that it was an easy evolutionary decision. Our lack of faith, while embarrassing, is common in many organizations because of the strong desire for status quo. Gratefully, our fears soon evaporated as the in-country team carried on fabulously.

Of course, it wasn't perfect. Many things still needed to be learned, and they were usually learned the hard way. Cultural differences became more apparent and frustrating. Our production of new water plants slowed. But in a reasonably short time, it became apparent that this was God's way of forcing us to pass the baton. It seems, at least for me, that many times we are frustrated while waiting for God's answers to prayers. After all, nothing we want ever comes fast enough for our human perceptions. This was a case where God was ready to move on and we were the ones frustrating Him!

These young men grew to become the core of our in-country support team. In addition to them, there were several key open boxes in the org chart that ultimately needed to be filled by other area men and women. While our Dominican org chart had more than a few open boxes, we determined that we would need each of the following going forward:

- Construction Crew to build the water plants – These jobs were typical developing world construction jobs that entailed site work, laying concrete block, mixing and pouring a concrete roof, installing doors and windows, etc.

- Credentialed Master Builder – This is a unique position required by the Dominican Republic government. Every construction site must have what they refer to as a Master Builder who has passed special schooling and a certification test, manages the effort, and is responsible for compliance to the many requirements the government has set.

- Technology Installation Specialist – This is a person that is responsible for installing all the components of our technology solution, and that can also develop a cursory knowledge of water science and its application within local situations.

- Electrician – Nearly every site we have ever worked at has issues with power. Typically it involves variable or limited amperage at a particular site. Employing a local person that is familiar with the unique power issues found in the developing world is essential to long term operations without pumps or technology components burning out.

- Community Relations – This person is responsible for helping the pastor or community leader develop a local marketing program that ensures successful water sales in the area. In order for the site to be successful, the local residents need to be certain the water is truly healthy, as well as regularly educated on the importance of clean water and sanitation.

- Evangelism Relations – Most local pastors have never had an asset to assist them in the growth of their congregations. The water plant, sited at the local church, is an exceptional resource. Help would need to be provided in developing water-related sermons, educational items for children, and specific programs to meet the needs of the residents.

- Water Testing Specialist – The guarantee that the technology we are implementing is continuously producing safe water to drink is critical to the sustainability of the site and Program. If the water ever fails, even just once, the trust of the community is jeopardized and sales could diminish significantly. As such, a Water Testing Specialist will need to travel to every site semi-monthly and test the water to ensure a great product that the residents can rely on.

Ultimately, it took considerable time to find local persons that could do the tasks required and accurately represent what Water@Work was all about. Every person is expected to learn and know their responsibility, but is also expected to provide community and evangelism support by their very nature and the way they interact with the residents. Every person representing Water@Work must first and foremost represent the love of Christ in their actions and communications.

Over time, local Dominicans or Haitians in the communities where water plants had been built were recruited. With rare exception, every member can readily explain the impact of the Program on the community they come from. All have experienced a personal spiritual awakening and come from places with unclean water. The testimonies offered by them to other locals are indeed powerful and has been responsible for many conversions.

Whereas in America a great resume is important to hiring decisions, a great heart is far more critical in the developing world. In nearly every instance, the people placed with the jobs described above had little or no direct experience. The exception is the specialist positions like Master Builder and Electrician. Even so, Water@Work was extremely committed to hire only local persons and improve the rampant unemployment in the places we served.

Even though no members of the team would sport what we would consider a great resume, we pay them like the professionals we expect them to be. This is made easier because of the extremely low wages typically paid in-country. Experienced construction personnel for instance would consider $5.00 per day a good wage. With little exception, we decided to double the local wages. While some would consider this extravagant, the financial impact due to the low wages was minor, and the benefit from zero employee turnover enabled us to really develop the skills of everyone on the team. Knowing a person will likely never want to leave the team lets us invest considerable amounts of time and education into every individual.

More Than a Drop in the Bucket?

Daniel Hidalgo Biya is one such recipient of this benefit. He has a family with four children and no education. He spent most of his time trying to get odd jobs that were never seemingly available. His family suffered tremendously from a lack of stable income. Even though he would spend every day in the community looking for any work, there was rarely any.

During the construction for a new water plant in a community called Villa Real, John noticed Daniel standing around watching the work for several days. Daniel finally approached John and asked if he could work for free and help with basic construction. Daniel quickly showed his ability for laying concrete block efficiently, and moved on to learn all aspects of a water plant's construction. He was paid in full for his work on the job and has been an integral part of the Water@Work in-country construction team ever since.

Because of his eagerness to learn and to do a great job, he has also been cross-trained in many areas. He has the pride that can only come from a stable career in honest labor. He sees a future that includes a new home for his family, and his children are getting the education that he was never blessed to have. His hard work has led to an incredible opportunity for his children to one day rise above their conditions. He is the very definition of hope in a hopeless place.

While some may argue that changing the future for one person like Daniel is just a proverbial drop in the bucket, Water@Work has seen differently. His success is infectious. The dozens employed in our In-Country Support Team all have similar stories. Success stories like these are rarely witnessed in poor rural communities and bateys. When even one is seen as an example, and the community develops from clean water and the introduction of commerce, everyone shares the hope. Good things start to happen and continue to snowball.

John is back home in Georgia now. But the anticipation of going back to the Dominican is never far from mind. He longs to return to his "boys" and the mission field. What he yearns for most, though, is "island time", or the relaxed nature of life, and the searching for "lost sheep". He deeply misses a lifestyle focused on at-risk youth eager to improve, and not continually the task at hand. Our focus here at home is to always be doing something and, in the process, we miss many personal opportunities. In the Dominican, the lifestyle encouraged looking beyond the accomplishment of tasks and centered more on the development of relationships.

With our organic but fledgling in-country organization developing, we were ready to implement our product in a limited roll-out and measure its effectiveness.

Life Lesson 9
When local people in the developing world are given a chance at success and led by the good Christian leaders, lasting development in local communities actually happens.

From John to you:

Bringing my family to the Dominican as missionaries has helped me get closer to God, my wife, my children and our "adopted guys." While at first it was one challenge after another, God is not in the habit of breaking people up over working in mission. He instead brought us even closer together as a family to serve Him.

Today I feel strengthened to go and serve wherever God needs me. I would encourage anyone to just GO! And don't focus on projects; focus on relationships.

10.   Every Instrument Needs Regular Tuning

> "All Scripture is breathed out by God and profitable for teaching, for reproof, for correction, and for training in righteousness…"
>
> *2 Timothy 3:16*

Smart businesses know that they need to re-engineer regularly or risk becoming stagnant. Even stoic companies that appear to never change continually fine-tune their operations to seek continuous improvement. In the late 1980s I was a team leader for the McDonnell-Douglas Corporation (now integrated into the Boeing Corporation), the huge airplane manufacturer and defense contractor. At the time, it employed more than 136,000 people. In those days, we called it Total Quality Management, and it was a major company initiative as witnessed by this statement from the Center for Excellence - Best Manufacturing Practices Award given to the company:

Continuous improvement requires a disciplined and focused process to address gaps that must be filled between the current state of operations and a desired end state. At MDA-St. Louis, this effort supported the PBM (Process Based Management) concept and the effective use of teams. Many tools have been developed to help implement this philosophy. Regular assessments and reports are produced to help management in its decision-making and budget allocation process… The key elements that make MDA-St. Louis' total quality management system work are the thoroughness and rigor with which it is pursued and the dedication of management in using the information provided by TQM assessment tools in making business decisions. The internal self-assessment uses the Malcolm Baldridge criteria.

The key elements are toughness and rigor leading to improved decision making. Put another way, it is essential for an organization's growth to actually attack the status quo. These are not academic exercises. They are instead formal and regular analysis made for the sole purpose of improving operations and product delivery.

If major corporations are driven to continually and creatively supply their products and services in more efficient and effective ways, then why should non-profits be any different? Certainly the end result is different, with one pursuing (essentially) profits while the other pursues (essentially) services, but one could argue that non-profits should be even more ambitious in continuous improvement programs. After all, if Boeing is inefficient in its product delivery model, the stock price falls and a lot of people lose some money.

If Water@Work is inefficient, people will suffer or die, and the gospel will not reach the thousands of ears ready to hear. Which would you pick as the most important? Of course it's the latter. And yet many non-profits fail to grasp this simple and powerful axiom. The result of which is manifested by increased suffering from those in need of service, frustration from those providing the service, and disappointment from those funding the service. A recent on-line post discussing this concept at Bible.org/The Learning Organization by Dr. Kenneth Boa states it well:

> *Continuous improvement requires continuous learning. Only the learning organization will, over the long haul, continue to grow. Paul provided the Colossian church with a marvelous insight into the concept of growth through learning:*

> *For this reason, since the day we heard about you, we have not stopped praying for you and asking God to fill you with the knowledge of his will through all*

spiritual wisdom and understanding. And we pray this in order that you may live a life worthy of the Lord and may please him in every way: bearing fruit in every good work, growing in the knowledge of God.
Colossians 1:9-10

The amount of money and cash-equivalents of human labor expended in the developing world in past decades measures in the many trillions of dollars. One would expect to find significant improvements after such significant investment. And yet when one travels the world, it's hard to find much evidence of true sustained development, and certainly not on par with that enormous investment. Clearly our delivery of services must change. While I would never suggest that Water@Work has solved the world's non-profit problems, I can state confidently that it actively challenged its model from every aspect imaginable to be as effective and creative as possible so that a positive difference could be measured and readily seen.

Create the Model, Break the Model, Repeat as Necessary

At Water@Work, we subscribe to the thinking that continuous improvement is imperative to the faithful stewardship of this ministry, and continuous improvement can only be achieved through continuous learning. This is accomplished in different ways and from different sources as the organization grows.

Continuous growth necessitates mentors that measure results, encourage teammates and facilitate improvement; not directors and managers that only observe results and finds flaws.

Early-stage organizations tend to focus inwardly, and Water@Work was no different. Our initial focus was on being internally responsible and as efficient as one could be with very limited resources. The lack of people and money to do what one knows needs to be done is both exasperating and vexing. To compensate, everyone pitches in and does the best they can. At one point or another, I have held the responsibilities of Founder, Executive Director, fund raiser, marketing person, website copywriter, implementation manager, logistics supervisor, and technology developer. Others in the organization have done similarly. All this, plus a full time job! Sounds impossible, right?

Not really. I was absolutely confident that our beginning, as humble as it was, had the anointing of our heavenly father. I was prayerfully certain that our efforts were lined up within His will and it would somehow happen. We'll continue on with how that happened, but first let's first meet another missional entrepreneur: Felix.

Felix lives in the Dominican Republic and has a heart for homelessness, which is rampant in the country. He started out just working all week and then going out on Friday and Saturday night to give the homeless a little food from his kitchen.

Soon he became a regular on the street and became noticed. The local newspaper liked the story and ran a short segment on his efforts in the paper. Because of my involvement in the country, I read the Dominican paper every day and happened upon the story. In it, he said that his dream was to have a home for the homeless because *there weren't any in the country.* I found it remarkable that a country with such a tremendous homeless problem could not even offer up one government sponsored place of shelter.

I contacted him the next day and asked him how I could help. He told me that he had a place picked out and an idea as to how he could manage. We went back and forth for many months as I tried to assess his true heart and the likelihood of success. In the end, our family worked with my brother's family to get him the money he needed. Then within days, a church in the State of Washington learned of his budding mission and agreed to send a missionary there to help him for a year!

And that's how it happens. God calls a person with a heart that shares His love, empowers that person through the Holy Spirit with the necessary energy, and Felix is on a path that seemed unimaginable just months prior.

It will not be easy for Felix. He and David, his missionary angel sent from the Washington church, will have to do everything right down to washing the dishes every night. His challenges will seem insurmountable as time goes on and his ministry matures. However, through a committed heart, lots of hard work, and the grace of an awesome God, he will certainly make a difference for the kingdom. As Margaret Mead, the celebrated cultural anthropologist eloquently noted:

> *"Never doubt that a small group of thoughtful, committed, citizens can change the world. Indeed, it is the only thing that ever has."*

As organizations mature their focus becomes more outwardly and they recognize their place in the community. One gets noticed and help generally arrives in the form of people and financial resources. Through the mantra of continuous learning and growth, organizations can manage the difficult climb to their goals. For Water@Work, over a period of two years the obstacles never seemed to end. Technical issues, government issues, fundraising issues, issues from issues, and then of course even more issues.

The good news is that with time and a remarkable group of people committed to the vision, all the issues fell like the dominoes our Dominican brothers play incessantly. Of course I'm not implying that we made it to Heaven while still on this earth. There are ALWAYS challenges and there ALWAYS will be challenges, but it definitely gets better.

The Path Has Many Potholes

Over time, Water@Work settled on a delivery model and end-product that fit all our requirements and goals. We had modified the model many times on the path towards finality, and the Dominican Republic had many sites of varying success where various different technical solutions and water plants could be seen.

Once the model was finalized, it took a great effort to go back and bring all the earlier sites up to the final standard. However, while we still only had a limited number of installed water plants, we became aware of one particularly serious flaw in the model that threatened to derail our entire effort. *The local residents in the bateys and poor rural communities (our end customers and the most important people in the process) didn't like the taste of the water!*

This took us completely by surprise. The water was incredibly healthy and full of minerals native to the island. The taste from the purification system is similar to well water many in the United States have. Unfortunately, that taste reminded them of the water in the ditches that made them sick. There was a powerful negative association between the taste of our clean healthy water and the taste of the water that made them sick.

Initially, we thought an education program could turn the tide. We could simply educate the consumers that the taste wasn't from the micro-organisms that made them sick, but instead from the minerals that made the water healthy. The ensuing endeavors were a great lesson in the power of local culture. Every effort ultimately failed miserably and the residents would have nothing of it.

Worse yet, the companies from the cities bottle de-ionized water, or water produced through the process of reverse-osmosis (RO). Many people around the world consume this type of water because it is the basis of virtually all bottled water available in the developed world. The big difference is that the bottled water we are used to has minerals added back into it prior to sale. Re-mineralized RO water contains certain minerals that make it healthier, but not enough to give it taste. Without the re-introduction of minerals, the water is considered unhealthy by many experts. While there are studies to dispute it, the World Health Organization, in its publication *"Health Risks from Drinking Demineralized Water,"* has condemned the practice of drinking straight RO water.

Let Me Tell You My Problems

One unfortunate reality in many organizations is perception that challenges are bad. Problems should be covered up or glossed over to maintain the status quo. One doesn't have to look beyond the daily paper to read of some organization or government hiding issues that lead to recalls, indictments, failures, cover-ups, and so forth. If one truly believes in continuous growth and the providence of a most-powerful God, challenges simply lead to better solutions.

At one of my company's staff meetings, I was complaining about this latest issue and how Water@Work was stymied by how to resolve it. Brandon Harper is a product specialist for the company who quietly does the work of a dozen and is totally committed to serving Christ with his life. In fact, he came to us after a career with Young Life, the very successful non-profit that minister to at-risk youth.

Many times, a fresh set of eyes on a situation can resolve more problems than all the internal people an organization can muster. Brandon came up with an elegant solution that could be implemented in the austere setting where we served. The simple solution was to continue using the Zeonic Filter system that produced clean mineralized water, but then blend it with an RO system. The result could then be adjusted to any mineral level that was acceptable. Basically, the individual water plant would start with de-ionized RO water and then mix in purified mineralized water to the maximum level until a taste was detected. They could then dial back the mineralized clean water a bit and nobody would taste it.

The process has since been branded by Water@Work as E-RO, or Enhanced Reverse Osmosis. This creative solution came from openly discussing challenges outside our organization and relying on

God to bring a solution. As it was in this case, it also provided the door that Brandon walked through to become an indispensable member of the ministry. Reducing the filter solution to just the Zeonic Filter and adding RO from a company that manufactures them in the Dominican Republic actually reduced our cost to implement significantly.

Thankfully, after making all the technical modifications we were at a place where we could roll out the model in-country. We could now deliver clean, healthy water within their specific cultural norms. We had made it to what we considered second base.

Life Lesson 10

Staying honest to your calling, vision and goals overcomes any challenge when we are acting within God's will.

From Brandon to you:

When I left my career with Young Life and went to work in the water purification industry, I was sad to see my chapter of ministry come to a close. With a young family, my time and finances were limited and I did not expect to be actively involved in an organization like Water@Work. God certainly had different plans.

I had traveled to the Dominican Republic several times before and been involved with development of the water purification equipment. As Water@Work expanded and began to face new challenges, God presented some very small opportunities for me to lend my ideas. By leaning into those small ideas, God allowed me to have a much larger part of the story than I ever could have expected. I believe that our journey with God is made up of many small steps of faith, rather than several giant leaps. That has been my experience with Water@Work, and I can only imagine where the next small steps will lead.

My prayer is that as Water@Work continues to grow, more and more people will have the opportunity to contribute to the mission. I pray that as my children grow up they will experience service to the developing world the way I have been able to.

Part 3

Growing the Baby

11. The Water@Work Model

"But remember the LORD your God, for it is he who gives you the ability to produce wealth, and so confirms his covenant, which he swore to your ancestors, as it is today."

Deuteronomy 8:18

After all the growing pains one could imagine, Water@Work settled into a business vision that met its core goals, reflected the needs of its customers, and satisfied the calling that God originally laid on my heart. The Three Big Drops we previously discussed that represented the pillars of the organization...

Healthy Bodies → Sustainability → Gospel Access

... morphed into a business model and operational perspective that truly captured everyone's considerations:

Dirty Water → Clean Water → Living Water

The above concise operational model was originally conceptualized by a team led by Mark Montonara, one of the most creative people I have ever worked with, and someone with a true knack for communications. Mark is actually one of the few paid contractors utilized by Water@Work. It is a testament to his heart that even though Water@Work can only afford a small stipend, his efforts approach full time involvement. Mark is at virtually every meeting and event, recording everything and turning it into web blogs, website content, organizational collateral, video development and any other form of communication one can imagine.

Mark believes that we best honor God by loving each other and trying to emulate the life that Christ showed us. To him the most important part of being a Christian is to walk in His steps as much as possible within our human limitations. While most Christians would agree with this, Mark recognizes that his ministry involvement offers the greatest opportunity to maximize the professional and spiritual gifts that God has given him.

The operational perspective above – Dirty Water to Clean Water to Living Water – directly drives the model from which the organization operates. While profound in its directness, we really just sought to emulate the model first demonstrated by our Lord while He was here among us. The Gospel accounts of the ministry of Christ often describe this powerful model. When He encountered a person in need, many times Christ first healed the body, then ensured the individual understood and could sustain over the long term, and lastly ministered to the soul by forgiving their sin. Healing of the physical being came before the healing of the heart. Water@Work simply adapted our Lord's example to the specific ministry and operations we work within.

Are We There Yet?

While it took significant effort and time to develop and expand the operational model, it became the measuring stick against which every decision was gauged. So let's explore each big operational drop more fully.

Dirty Water: As is witnessed in most parts of the world, the areas where we serve in the Dominican Republic suffer greatly from water-borne illness. In one batey that had a clinic and doctor, 91% of all cases he saw one year were from water-borne illness. While that number is staggering, it provided assurance that we were on the right path. Resolving this one health issue could greatly impact the development of the community and the individuals living there.

The critical need for clean water starts with the babies and children. Parasites in unhealthy water can cause incredible pain, significant dehydration from diarrhea, and eventually death. The parasites actually consume the food eaten by the child before the child can process it. The worms in their stomachs and intestines grow and distend the stomach while the child literally starves.

Adults that contract a water-borne disease can typically outlast the diarrhea if clean water becomes available. However, any time lost from work can lead to their losing their jobs and homes. The bateys are full of adults without work because they got sick and were summarily fired by the companies they worked for. With so many willing to work for incredibly meager wages, there is near zero tolerance for sickness. Older and aged adults are also highly susceptible to water-borne illness, and with increased age come the greater likelihood of death from the diseases.

Clean Water: The world is riddled with water purification systems that were installed in some place with great need, only to become broken and unused in a very short time. As with any machinery, over time a water purification system needs to be maintained properly to continue working. Filters and UV bulbs need to be replaced, and membranes need to be cleaned. Or, as we actually experienced at one of our sites, a donkey gets loose, kicks a pipe and breaks it. As a person from the developed world, try getting that message one day in the thick of life and not chuckling. Without regular maintenance, such frequent occurrences can render highly expensive pieces of equipment worthless.

Water@Work was adamant that it would be good stewards of its donations and make sure the resources for a sustainable clean water system were always there. The costs to provide the professional support organization we envisioned had to be accounted for in the basic model. However, the source of these funds cannot ultimately come from America or any organization outside the community.

It was paramount to us that the model enabled sustainability from the local community and nobody else. At some point, all good-meaning organizations can no longer allocate the funds to maintain the systems they have put in place. The result is countless purification systems that have ceased to operate properly and are eventually pilfered for parts.

Living Water: This area was critical to Water@Work. The poor communities and bateys where we serve are greatly afflicted by both spiritual apathy and voodoo. Apathy towards God comes from the daily focus on survival and bleak outlook for the future. This was the one thing that really stuck with Mark after his first trip in-country.

He has noted that he cannot imagine the courage it takes just to face every day under the local conditions. Yet there were those that hold tight to their faith through immeasurable hardship. His comments remind me of my first mission trip where we attended Pastor Pedro's church. I sat in back of an older gentleman that clutched his heart and was pleading with God throughout most of the service. With one hand on his chest and another raised to God, he prayed, complained, and yelled in such an intensive manner that I couldn't help but weep at length. Initially, I prayed for him. Then I soon started to pray for forgiveness for myself.

Because of where I live and my lifestyle, I had never prayed like that. Anyone in America is affluent compared to those we serve, and affluence makes a person falsely feel secure. It subsequently reduces our fear of the Lord and wrongfully emboldens self-reliance. Have you ever secretly thought to yourself when times are going well that "I have this covered", like I have? Sure you have.

But instead of this approach, this gentleman was relying totally on God – for everything – and I was to some degree always relying on myself. Even in my worst of times, even as I gave a particular problem over to God, it is difficult to claim the closeness with God that that stranger had.

It would be tremendous to say that this gentleman represented the many. Unfortunately, it is just the opposite and the harvest field is enormous. In addition to the daily struggle for life, the people are more likely to encounter voodoo than the Gospel. The insidious perversion that is voodoo is very common and the people are greatly influenced by its practice. One of the primary reasons for focusing on the Dominican Republic bateys and poor rural communities is because there is such a great need to spread the Gospel good news message.

Water is actually a tremendous medium for spreading the gospel. There are many verses in the bible referencing water or its value. The linking of our human message for good health and hygiene through *clean water* with the heavenly message of eternal life through Christ the *Living Water* is easy to communicate and meaningful.

Water@Work has been committed from the very beginning to using the water systems to spread the Gospel. It was actually the driving force behind the name; the *water* is *at work* to bring the Gospel and good health to those in need.

Viva la Difference!

The Water@Work model is truly unique in many ways. It has been borne from years of trials and earnest prayer. It is also the result of listening to our customers every step of the way. There were many times when it was necessary to change our processes or structure to meet the requirements of the people we serve and their culture.

> *All successful business models are focused on their customers. In the world of non-profits, the organization absolutely must change, adapt, modify, and do whatever is required to conform to the expectations of its customer.*

The cultural component of any international ministry cannot be overstated. Mark would certainly agree. He was amazed while in-country that it didn't take long to look beyond the poor country one easily sees, and instead absorb the rich culture one experiences. While the culture many times takes on a humorous tone or makes one stop in their tracks and scratch their head, the underlying cultural realities must be respected for the model to fully succeed.

Part of that reality is that that the rest of the world simply does not think or act like Americans. In many cases, the societal norms have been established for hundreds or even thousands of years and, no matter how illogical or inconvenient to us, will not change. As adaptability generally leads to increased cost and effort, it becomes easy to assume the customer will change. That mistake is incredibly common and can be witnessed by the many organizations that never gain traction or are not trusted in-country.

Reflecting many years of in-country lessons learned and key relationships nurtured, the essence of the Water@Work model can be summarized as follows:

1. Find a great community in need. Identify a community that has a high likelihood of success. This includes parameters affecting both technology suitability and fitting demographics that will ensure sustainability.

   Visit the location to complete the following forms and subjectively identify any factors that lends to a positive or negative perspective on the community. Help the community complete and submit a *Program Application Form*.

   Complete a *Site Assessment Form*, including general community and demographic information, current community water and health situation, community resources, and financial factors such as ability of the residents to pay a very small amount for the water.

   Complete a *Project Cost Estimation Form*, including any cost mitigation factors such as resources already on site, extra construction requirements, or any items that affect the cost either upward or downward.

2. Identify a local pastor or leader of a community Christian organization with vision for the community. – The pastor is arguably the most important component of the process. He or she must fully understand and accept their responsibility to lead the community in its development. The sales of water will not

only provide the monies to ensure its sustainability, but also generate a profit that must be spent to benefit and grow the church and community.

Profits are typically allocated to building schools, paying teachers, developing agriculture programs, or whatever the church and community deem in its best interest. Water@Work monitors the use of the funds, but does not ex-patriate the money back to America or keep any part of it. In this way the church and its leaders have the resources for "home-grown" development that can be sustained without continually coming back looking for additional funds.

3. Conduct marketing within the community to raise excitement. Water@Work has developed several marketing efforts that serve to develop a "buzz" in the community. This excitement for the availability of clean water is important to begin the education process on the importance of clean water and hygiene. Over time it is intended for this effort to be maximized even further.

4. Build a water plant adjacent to the church. The water plant is actually built on the church property so people have to, literally, go to church for their clean water. Importantly, the water plant positions the church as the reason for their good health and improved economic position. The positive association between the clean water and the living water of Jesus can then be reinforced daily as the people come for their water.

5. Donate the water plant to the local church. The water plant is officially donated to the church. This is significant because in these communities there is very little actually owned by anyone. The pride of ownership for the church and community residents is incredible to witness and extremely important towards future community development.

6. Conduct a Training Class. A training class is conducted for the pastor and a team of local residents. These trained individuals will be responsible for the daily operations of the E-RO equipment and water plant.

7. Sign a *Support Contract*. The Support Contract is a binding document that ensures Water@Work will provide personnel and equipment to maintain the technology in good working order and warrants the total system. The cost for this is very small and taken from the water sales within and outside the community.

8. Issue *Training Certificates*. Training Certificates are issued to all that successfully complete the class so that residents can be confident that the equipment operators are certified as capable.

9. Conduct a community blessing service. The blessing service is a great way for the community to thank God for the blessing of the water plant and all it will mean in their lives. It is also a great mechanism to kick off of the evangelism component of the model.

10. Begin water sales and continue community marketing. It is typical that in the first month or so, the church gives free water to the residents. This gives everyone in the community and surrounding areas the opportunity to taste the great water. Actual sales of the water begin at some point determined by the church and community. The price for the water is determined by the community and typically equates to about $0.25 to $0.50 per five gallon jug. This is quite a savings from the average price of $1.00 to $2.00 charged in the cities, assuming some of the residents can afford to buy a jug occasionally.

    The savings not only mean that virtually everyone can afford it, but the increase in family income by the residents will enable them buy food or other essentials. If a family cannot even afford this low cost, then the church has the discretion to give the family its water for free. Charging for the water is critical to having the model succeed, but nobody wants any family that truly can't afford it to go without.

11. Evaluate your success. Water@Work strives to provide significant accountability to its organization and donors. It measures a great many things to gauge growth and success.

As part of its warranty and support service, Water@Work sends a local representative regularly to test the water for efficacy. The representative documents the findings and ensures a consistently good source of water that the community can count on. While on site, any beneficial maintenance is also completed to ensure that proper procedures for the production of clean water and government regulations are adhered to.

Lastly, it is required as a term of the Support Agreement that the church logs its water sales. This information is typically maintained locally in notebooks and then uploaded to America and entered into spreadsheets so the sales history can be followed. The process serves as accountability for the local church and its employees against potential water sales theft.

12. Coordinate a regular Best Practices Conference. As the number of water plants grew and a critical mass ensued, Water@Work hosted a conference that was open to any pastor or community leader that had a water plant. The Conference was very successful and provided an excellent networking experience for pastors from across the country that do not see each other often. It is anticipated that these conferences will be conducted on a regular basis to exchange best practices and provide a vehicle for the pastors to share their marketing and business successes.

Some creative examples of how the churches are expanding their businesses include using the clean water to make liquid soap and cleaning supplies that then is sold, as well as selling the clean water to local farmers so produce can be rinsed with clean water before shipping. It is truly amazing to see how creative these souls become when they have an asset and some basic help in maximizing it.

Ultimately, the Water@Work model is just that: an over-arching model. It produces a "product" with varied "customers" that view the product from different perspectives. We will soon discuss how this critically impacts the organization and its operations. But first, there was just one more critical expansion and modification of the model that provided for greater growth and lower costs.

Life Lesson 11

Given proper resources and a helping hand, the developing world can actually develop - and the church can be its catalyst.

From Mark to you:

I feel so humbled to be just a small part of the work that is being done through this ministry. I believe that Water@Work is certainly a true expression of Christ's message to love one another through acts of love and compassion.

I am personally lifted up by the experience. To know the impact that this ministry's work has, it makes the work of communicating the message of the ministry's work so enjoyable and satisfying. How can you not want to get up each day to do your job when your job is let people know of the good work that is going on in Christ's name for those less fortunate.

There are many people with talents and resources that can help spread the message of ministry projects like Water@Work Ministry. I would invite those who have these talents to make a commitment to contributing to help build up God's Kingdom somewhere – it could be in your backyard or on the other side of the world. Whatever the distance, the reward will be waiting for you.

12. Just One More Tweak to the Model...

"As they sat down to eat their meal, they looked up and saw a caravan of Ishmaelites coming from Gilead. Their camels were loaded with spices, balm and myrrh, and they were on their way to take them down to Egypt."

Genesis 37:25-28

I've come to learn that some of the worst mistakes I have ever made involved words or thoughts that went along the lines of *"wow, we are really doing well"*, or *"I think we are ready to sit back and really roll this out."* Don't get me wrong... it is not wrong to assess where one is and feel a satisfaction that things are going well. But as soon as a semblance of complacency sets in, God seems to consider it good sport to throw a wrench in the works. While these generally end up being correcting moves from God that you learn to be grateful for, it just sometimes would be nice for a breather.

No such luck. At the end of 2014, Water@Work was a few years old and really hitting full stride. We had a terrific team of people both in-country and domestically that lived and breathed our mission. Our truly unique model was working very well in the Dominican Republic. Many local in-country pastors were being incredibly successful and creative. At communities that were blessed with a water plant, water-borne disease was a thing of the past, community development projects were moving forward, and many lives were coming to Christ.

Much of the year was spent developing a healthy relationship with the Dominican government and putting in all the mechanisms and requirements that they needed in order for our sites to be considered "legal". Never mind that many of these requirements seemed onerous and achieved little except to increase our costs.

These included such expensive and unnecessary things as requiring the water plants to have air conditioning even though the windows would stay open when water was for sale, or having to tile not only the floors, but all the walls in the plant as well, and more than a few others.

The positive of the effort was their acknowledgement that we were producing significantly healthier water than commonly available, and doing it in places not generally serviced. This proved to be a considerable achievement. The government went from antagonist to friend, and with it came much better communication and coordination. It also led to their decision that our testing lab was acceptable for their regulatory requirements. As such, we didn't need to have a third party provide testing documentation for the government. We could simply test our own water in our lab and save significantly in both cost and time perspectives. While other water projects from US non-profits were being categorized as "illegal" sites, the government was helping us with the elimination of import taxes and tariffs, the selection of sites with a high likelihood of success, anti-corruption efforts, and more.

Unfortunately, all of the improvements to the model had produced a cost per site that left some donor organizations unable to fund a full water plant by themselves. One might reasonably assume that multiple churches, civic groups or individuals would be happy to cooperate and merge funds to achieve a successful project. In reality though, if possible, most would prefer to be responsible for the project from start to finish, particularly if they are sending mission teams in-country to work on the project.

It would have been very easy to stay with the existing model that worked so well, but constant improvement demands re-engineering any process that can improve service or better steward resources.

So while we were gratefully being funded with significant amounts from larger churches, smaller churches and individuals weren't participating as fully as hoped for. This was a concern because we truly desired a reality where the entire body of Christ could participate in the ministry. But the even bigger concern was ensuring that everyone in need could be served. Many smaller bateys and rural communities have less than a hundred families, while others with as few as a dozen families regularly spring up around the country. Developing a high-end water plant in these smaller communities simply didn't compute from the perspectives of both initial cost and long term support.

What about the Little Guys?

There was a point when we all realized that the cost to build a full water plant with all the necessary technology in smaller communities simply couldn't be justified. While we intuitively knew this unsettling reality, we easily deferred serious conversation on it to instead focus on the more immediate goal of rolling out a critical mass of successful water plants. Remember how we earlier got in trouble by doing what felt good instead of adjusting the model? Well, that's a toughie that we nearly fell victim to again.

Fortunately, while we were plugging away and feeling good about the number of water plants we were building, some of our in-country customers didn't just see the need - they felt it. They recognized the responsibility to provide the smaller communities with the same clean water blessings they were experiencing, and they wanted to help. One such pastor was Juan Osvalvo Vilorio Polanco of the Evangelical Church of the Dominican Republic, a church located in the Magante community on the north side of the island. He took it upon himself to independently try supporting those communities near him, and his bold actions eventually led to a major modification in our model.

But before exploring this change, we need to recognize a hard under-current reality that plagues most non-profits...Water@Work included. Because we serve "them," at a generally unspoken plane, we consider them in a situation beneath "us." No matter the service provided, we rarely look to those we serve first for the solution to the problems encountered in *their* reality. While this superiority complex is rarely overtly voiced, it runs under the surface everywhere. I'm sure many reading this would profess differently, but it is a sad reality in even the best run organizations.

The developed world has the money and education and, at some level, believes we hold the keys to creative problem solving. When encountering a problem, how often do any of us really first go to those we serve for the solution or opinion? How many organizations have those they serve on their Boards or in positions of decision making? The lack of respect we show those we serve and these subtle feelings of superiority are shameful and certainly not Christ-like. At Water@Work we resolve to be consciously alert to this natural tendency and to snuff it out as we occasionally fall victim to it.

That is why it was such a joy and revelation to have a local Dominican pastor show us the solution to a problem that we wrongfully thought we needed to resolve for them. Pastor Vilorio's community is on a nicely paved main road with enough traffic to generate great water sales. However, just a few hundred feet from the road the mountain starts, and it is the home to many smaller bateys without electricity or running water. Most vehicles cannot make it up the gravel and dirt jungle openings that are euphemistically referred to as "roads." This is particularly true when it rains which, in this part of the island, is virtually every day.

Pastor Vilorio had estimated that he could pay for fuel and maintenance costs for a delivery vehicle to bring these communities water, but not for the cost of the vehicle itself. After significant prayer by his entire church community, they located a small propane powered delivery vehicle that would be perfect for the narrow and rough pathways to these smaller villages. Their prayers were answered when a church in the United States donated the funds to acquire the vehicle. In short order Pastor Vilorio had the crude beginnings of a distribution system that could work within his in-country realities.

Most non-profits talk a lot about "coming alongside" the people they serve, or "giving a hand-up instead of a hand-out." But the reality is that Americans think like Americans. We generally try with the best of intentions to experience local realities and get as close as possible as often as possible. Unfortunately, we are all victims of the paradigms we live in. For all the many months and, in the case of our missionaries, many years that we work in-country, it is still easy to assign a committee to a problem and just go at it. It takes discipline to honestly rely upon the truth that the best source of innovation lies with them.

This certainly was true in Magante, and working together produced a tweaking of our model that has made a huge difference for both ourselves and our customers. The creativity and desire to serve demonstrated by Pastor Vilorio was more than convicting. It was the spark that drove some major improvements.

The Wheel is Still Perfect

One could easily argue that the wheel is the most significant human achievement in history. At least as a retired engineer, I would certainly argue it. In addition to its astounding functionality and myriad uses, it has also given inspiration to businesses that utilize its "hub and spoke" nature to deliver all sorts of goods and services. One does not have to look far to see this exemplified. From the airline industry to food distributors, the efficiencies gained by the hub and spoke concept are significant.

As Fabrizio Dallari of the Libero Instituto Universitario Carlo Cattaneo summarizes in the Journal of Physical Distribution & Logistics Management: *"The Hub and Spoke system (H&S), initially applied to the airline industry, is an innovative distribution approach which has proved to be successful especially in transportation systems dealing with several origins and destinations..."* The following figures taken from his work effectively describe this.

Figure 1 below is a description of the way airlines at one time flew from point to point among independent, discreet destinations.

It required a significant number of aircraft and resulted high costs to operate and an inefficient method of servicing many locations. Most regrettably, it could not produce enough efficiency to service smaller markets. Persons desiring a flight in smaller cities would have to drive to the larger cities where there was service. This is very much akin to our reality with the smaller Dominican communities.

Figure 1 – Independent Destination Airline Model

Conversely, Figure 2 below depicts the same delivery of service to all the desired locations but in a much more efficient manner, utilizing far less resources. The savings in this delivery model resulted in many smaller destinations obtaining service, but also a savings in costs because of a reduction in the number of planes required to deliver the service and their maintenance.

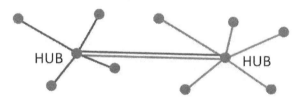

Figure 2 – Improved Hub and Spoke Based Model

This service delivery improvement is extremely close to the opportunity present in trying to distribute water amongst the many bateys. It seemed fitting that our model could realize cost reduction and improved access by drawing inspiration from the hub and spoke concept. Based upon the lessons learned from Pastor Vilorio and other in-country experiences, Water@Work endeavored to develop its own version.

Figure 3 below shows the historical Water@Work model that relied on a completely independent water plant built at each discrete batey. In this model, each location was outfitted with a complete water plant, including all the necessary and expensive construction and testing realities required to ensure government compliance.

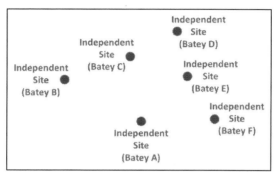

Figure 3 – Historical Water@Work Model

To completely realize the vision of bringing clean water and the gospel to all the poor rural communities in the country, an exceptionally significant increase in funding and many decades of time would be required. Equally daunting was that a considerably larger in-country support team would be required to ensure water quality and community development at the additional several hundred sites. The expansion and management of the potential effort made us cringe. In addition to the operational impact of such an expansion, its cost would also consume community water sales revenues that could instead be used for important community development and evangelism projects.

Figure 4 below depicts the expanded Water@Work model. It features a Hub Site with a full-scale water plant that then disseminates its water via delivery vehicles on a regular schedule to people and churches in smaller communities. For those communities that are larger, yet too small for a full Hub Site, small distribution buildings at a local church may be constructed.

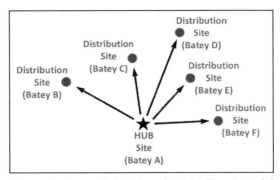

Figure 4 – Expanded Hub and Spoke Based Model

The cost advantage to the improvement shown in the model was considerable. Significantly, it also led to the wonderful realization that the vision of the organization could be achieved much sooner than ever thought before. While a great many Hub Sites still needed to be built, many smaller communities could now be served and they could realize all the blessings previously available only in the larger communities.

Linear Growth vs. Exponential Growth

One of the core goals of Water@Work was to mobilize the body of Christ to come together to eliminate thirst, promote community development, and improve access to the Gospel of Christ for its vulnerable population in an entire country. In the Dominican Republic, that means about 350 bateys and rural communities housing approximately 1,500,000 persons.

By the end of 2014, some 27 full system water plants were either completed or under construction. To put a complete full scale water plant into every batey could certainly be accomplished, but the cost would be many millions of dollars and take a very long time. This is the linear growth that was historically pursued.

However, with the adoption of the newly implemented Hub and Spoke model, growth really had the potential to accelerate. The only realized cost to deliver water to smaller sites is the delivery vehicle because fuel and operating costs are covered by water sales. Even when a Distribution Site Building is required due to a larger number of families in the community, one could be built at approximately 67% less than the cost of a Hub Site. This equates to about three constructed Distribution Site Buildings for the same general cost as one Hub Site. If one considers the many smaller communities served directly from the truck and not needing a distribution building, the total number of communities served by one Hub Site can easily increase to six or more.

Not only were we now positioned for exponential growth, but a significantly greater number of donor organizations and individuals could participate as well. Smaller churches and individuals that could not previously fund an entire Hub Site could independently afford to fund evangelism and support efforts, a Delivery Vehicle, or Distribution Site Building. While the funding cost to implement the traditional model was always very low, the end cost to produce and deliver a five gallon jug of water was now reduced to a fraction of a penny.

More importantly to our mission, the distribution of the clean water also facilitates church planting. As smaller communities are served with clean water, the people come to know the distributing church and those representing it with their delivery. Over time, the impact of the church into these smaller communities generally leads to the planting of both bible study groups and full scale churches. While church planting is not a distinct part of the Water@Work mission, it is yet another tremendous benefit that comes from the church ownership and management of the clean water plants and the model.

The improvement to the model was also significant in many ways beyond those discussed. Perhaps most significantly, it was led by a customer in a local community. The initial boldness from Pastor Vilorio educated us to respect the creativity and problem-solving skills of those we serve. Since this first awakening, we have found that creativity is typical of the many great local leaders in these poor rural communities. Time and again these communities have proven that they will succeed when provided with the required tools and support.

With all its maturations and tweaks, the Water@Work model is never considered done or complete. It did, however, reach a point where additional major improvements slowed considerably. Further, any such modifications flowed almost entirely from our attempts to meet the expectations of both our customers and donors, as you'll see in the coming chapters.

Life Lesson 12
Just when you think you have "it" all working well, there is always a way to make "it" better.

From Pastor Vilorio to you:

The gift of the water plant has given us the chance to move beyond our current conditions. We have to be creative with our problems. The clean water we now make gives us many chances to be creative with our problems.

Water@Work has been very helpful to us as we build our business. Through it, we are reaching many people with clean water for a healthy life and the living water of Christ Jesus. We also see many improvements in our community now. Thank you to everyone that has made this possible for us. Our communities will always be very grateful.

13. Meeting Customer Expectations

> *"As it is my eager expectation and hope that I will not be at all ashamed, but that with full courage now as always Christ will be honored in my body, whether by life or by death."*
>
> Philippians 1:20

As we have discussed previously, every non-profit organization produces a product, even if they prefer not to think of it that way. They are in the business of providing some service, assistance, or physical item(s) that an end user is in need of and grateful for. In this Chapter we will discuss the Water@Work product from the unique perspective of its end customers and their expectations. In actuality, the Water@Work customer base is really segmented into three types of persons that each has different expectations.

Customer Type 1 – The Community Resident

This is by far our most important customer. Without their acceptance of the water that the churches produce, the entire model breaks down. But even within this customer segment there are really three types of end users that have different needs, and each must receive commensurate value.

The children of the community: The children of the bateys rarely attend school in the manner Americans are accustomed to. Schooling in the poor rural communities is very limited and typically ends at grade three. For example, Renata is a young girl living in a batey, about the age of eleven. When I first met her, she had only gone to school for three years in a building that was re-purposed after being previously abandoned. When the make-shift school could not afford teachers, she took it upon herself to teach the little ones basic math and how to write their names. It is quite humbling to see a classroom of about fifty very small children being taught math by an eleven year old using small stones and sticks as props!

The dream of her community was to get a water plant that could provide the funds for teachers and an expanded school. The expectation of Renata, like most children in the bateys, is simply consistently clean water that provides the opportunity to grow without the constant threat of water-borne illness. Going to school and having an opportunity to break the cycle of extreme poverty would be icing on the cake. By the grace of God however, her community eventually made that a reality by getting a Water@Work Water Plant. Building schools or paying for teachers and supplies is a common goal of the communities that Water@Work serves.

> *By any measure, a local person with a healthy body, proper education and a desire to serve Christ and community, will do more to promote true development than any government could hope to do.*

Renata is typical of how the children grow up fast in these areas. Gratefully, she has accepted Christ and one day hopes to be a teacher and Christian leader. The last time I spoke with her, I asked where she would like to live. She responded that her prayer was to one day go to the city and college, but then return to her batey. She is certain that one day a school will materialize from the monies her community is saving from the new water sales and she wants to play a significant role. Truly an inspiring young woman!

The adults of the communities: While less susceptible to life-threatening waterborne illness as children because of matured bodies, adults still require healthy water so they can work in the tobacco, coffee, or sugar cane fields. Those fortunate enough to have work do so at extremely low wages. While no official numbers are available, independent sources reveal a daily wage of about $1.00. Getting sick and missing even a day of work can mean the end of a job that may take years to recover from.

Armando has fallen victim to this. His parents had come from Haiti to the Dominican as employees of the sugar cane company. Unfortunately, the children of such immigrants lack proper citizenship papers from Haiti and are denied Dominican citizenship.

They are considered *persona-non-grata*, meaning unwelcome or unwanted persons in the country. Armando began cutting cane at the age of twelve and continued until he had a minor accident in the fields. While one would not expect a cut to result in a major loss of work, an infection brought on by contaminated water used to treat the wound ensued.

Not able to work in the fields any longer, he has spent the second half of his life working odd jobs when he could find one. When forced to go extended periods without work, he resorts to begging to provide for his children. For Armando, the very low cost of clean water means he can not only afford it for his family, but he can now free up some money to have more consistently healthy foods. For adult residents of the bateys, the expectations are primarily that the clean water will result in some additional monies for other necessities, as well as good health to continue working.

Customer Type 2 – The Community Church and Pastor

The churches or Christian Centers that are blessed with a water plant have a significant responsibility and resultant high expectations from us. They understand that they are the hope for their community. Through their stewardship the community will have its first and likely only owned asset. The residents will be blessed with good health, additional income, and important community developments. Without it and effective leadership though, decades more may pass without any real development or hope.

Most pastors in the rural communities have small churches that meet in huts or run-down buildings. Their congregations are typically a couple dozen people and rarely exceed fifty. It is incredibly difficult to grow a church in such dire places where the focus of life is simply survival.

Most of the pastors have been led to preach by the Spirit and are not formally trained or have an appropriate education. For many, learning to read the Bible has been the extent of their education. However, without exception, each is driven to make a difference in the people and community they serve. For the proper candidate, a donated water plant is their best vehicle to move the local church and community forward.

The pastors in these fortunate churches must evolve from pastors with limited congregants to business leaders and pastors of growing churches. Pastor Alejandro Guzman is just such a person. He is the pastor in Batey San Juaquin, a particularly difficult batey that had little hope.

There was a gathering spot by a local bar where prostitution was rampant. Everyone for miles knew to come there for drugs, liquor, and the poor girls of the batey with no other hope for income except prostitution. Pastor Alejandro had a vision to buy the property and build a church there. He was certain the message of Christ would reach these, the most vulnerable souls there.

His prayers were answered when a church in America donated the funds to buy the land and build a church. Water@Work responded by funding the water plant. Within a year, this place of spiritual and physical death became the source of life and the future. In a tangible way, the people of the batey saw God triumph over evil and the batey quickly exhibited many signs of positive growth.

The water plant is the spark of hope and development for of their community. Pastor Alejandro has the expectation that his technology will operate effectively and consistently. The water sales are the mechanism that will fuel the growth, and its operation must be reliable. He is typical of churches that are blessed with water plants in that he now has a list of development projects they are saving towards. In addition to ensuring his technology is operating properly, Water@Work has also helped him with their community development plans.

More importantly, he has seen his church membership swell since he started providing safe water to the community. The local residents clearly see how the church has helped them in a very real way while the government and companies that control the community do virtually nothing. The den of prostitution and every form of vice have been replaced by a house of God. One cannot argue the change that is apparent there and throughout the community.

Pastor Pedro, whom we met earlier, is another pastor but with a larger church and small school in an urban area on the other side of the country close to the Haiti border. His dream was to open an orphanage to house the many homeless children that seem to be everywhere. Through funding from his congregants and churches in America, he was able to finally build the orphanage that can house one hundred children.

Unfortunately, the funds to keep the orphanage operating and pay for the church and school did not continue over time. This is unfortunately common, as donors leave projects to move on to other projects. Sustaining funds seem to *always* be the problem.

Water@Work installed a water plant in between the church and the orphanage. Pastor Pedro now produces enough clean water to provide the children of the school and the orphanage all they need, *and* still have enough to sell as much as he can to the community.

The church saves money by not having to buy water for the school and orphanage at high city prices, and they make enough in sales to satisfy the Support Agreement and fund some of the continuing orphanage operations cost.

These two examples of pastors and churches using the water plants to change their communities and expand access to the Gospel of Christ typify the best of what Water@Work is, and how seismic changes can occur from humble efforts ordained by an awesomely powerful God.

Customer Type 3 – The Donor Customer

None of the benefits discussed up to now could happen without donors in America stepping forward to fund the ministry. Their unselfish giving is the backbone of any success Water@Work can possibly achieve. This is also the case with most non-profits, yet many do little to recognize that the donor has expectations that go beyond simply getting a thank you.

Most donors appreciate being kept abreast of more than just activities or fund raisers. They also appreciate honest communications on how things are going in the organization and on the specific project or, in our case, the specific comunity they may be interested in. The communication is positive and it feels good to share the successes achieved.

However, working in the developing world is rife with issues. The logistics of moving equipment to a foreign country, building major structures, installing high end technology in places with little resources, dealing with water pressure and insufficient power issues, and establishing commerce in places where there is none mean delays, setbacks, and many things Americans hate to hear about.

While it can be painful, we have found that having donors not knowing what is going on is more harmful than sharing the truth of what may be happening at a particular site. Gratefully, every major donor that comes to mind has generally been patient, sees beyond short-term issues, and thinks long-term.

Of course, there are many times when things go smoothly. As the organization matures and if one is blessed with stability of staff, the issues will typically become less significant and frequent. Whatever the news, good or bad, honest communications is imperative towards developing donor relations that last.

Equally important are the frequency with which donors are communicated with and their preferred method of communication. We found that asking our customers how often they wanted to be updated and kept in contact with was very positive. Additionally, because different people like to communicate in different methods, their preferred communication method is important. For example, some prefer a phone call on occasion, while others simply want an email.

There is only one boss...the customer. And he can fire everybody in the company from the chairman on down, simply by spending his money somewhere else.

- Sam Walton

Most important is having something real to communicate. Just "going back to the well" and asking for more money generally doesn't cut it. Some of our donors are excited by the evangelism component of our work. Namely, how many more baptisms are there after a water plant goes in? Or how has the congregation grown in members? Others are more interested in the community development side of our model and want to know the status of schools being built or jobs being created.

Whatever the end product is, communicating to donors is paramount. This can be very difficult for non-profits, but every attempt has to be made. Donors want to hear about how their gift has made a difference in the areas that excite them via communication methods that they prefer. Not an easy task to be sure!

While we are never satisfied with the status quo in this regard, here are some of the methods Water@Work has developed to communicate with its donors:

- Outward Technology: Outward technology encompasses all the non-personal communications sent out via social media like Facebook, Twitter, LinkedIn, etc., as well as general email blasts. These types of communication typically provide current situations, general status and notifications of events and such.

- Inward Technology: Inward technology utilizes the website, www.wateratworkministry.org, to provide current status on operations and particular projects. For example, we provide an interactive map of the country showing all the locations that have a water plant, those that are in the construction process, and those we are seeking funding for. A donor or interested party can find out the status of the implementation they helped fund, learn about a community seeking a water plant, or identify a community they may wish to support all by simply selecting the icon on the map at any time.

- Personal Involvement: For most of the old-schoolers, nothing beats a personally communicated thank you. At Water@Work every donation receives a communication that includes a thank you and tax receipt. But for those of a certain amount or higher, the donor receives a hand written note and/or phone call expressing our thanks. Donors with a significant involvement get regular personal visits to ensure they are updated on both the status of our organization and the status of the community or communities they are supporting.

As we have seen, each of the customer groups has a different need from our end product. Each customer must have their expectations met and receive commensurate benefits for the model to be successful. Proper communication to our customer groups necessitates good communications with our in-country team.

Life Lesson 13

It's easy and expected to lean on internal organizational expectations but when serving Christ, all efforts need to focus on the expectations of those being served.

From Pastor Alejandro to you:

Nothing here ever seemed to change and every day was like the last. Now, we see change all the time – in the community and in people's lives. I can't measure how much the water plant has meant to us, but it is very large. From babies sleeping all night to new community projects, so many lives here have been changed!

God bless you for caring about us in a way that is so large we cannot measure.

14. Meeting Accountability Expectations

> *"So then each of us will give an account of himself to God."*
>
> *Romans 14:12*

Accountability can mean different things to different people. It is often really a matter of perspective. From a personal perspective we are accountable to our spouses, children, extended families, and so on. From a professional perspective, we are accountable to supervisors, employers, customers, and the like. Water@Work seeks to have accountability at virtually every critical component of its model. While this is an expense that often becomes significant, it is imperative to ensuring good stewardship of the time, talents and treasures of every person in the organization and its customers.

It is one thing to say something is working, but quite another to quantify specific results. The closer one gets to the customer, the easier it becomes to be more measured. Earlier in the process, results are rarely exact and are instead far more nebulous and subjective. A typical example is provided, with a more specific accountability question following:

- The typical – We want to build water plants in the eastern side of the island.
    - ✓ The more accountable – What is the distribution of sites in each of the four island regions, and why?

- The typical – We have seen a lot more people coming to church.
    - ✓ The more accountable – What are the monthly attendance figures since implementation of the water plant?

- The typical – Costs on water plant Y were a bit high, but pretty close to plan.
  - ✓ The more accountable – What was the over-run amount, why, and will we see this additional cost elsewhere in the future?

- The typical – They should start selling water at community Z so on
  - ✓ The more accountable – Are they selling according to plan and, if not, how can the reason for delay be mitigated in the future, and so on?

Measurement becomes more objective typically down the road in the process. Many times in early stage organizations it is simply not known what to ask about. Not enough progress has been made in the model to know where the critical areas and potential points of failure are. The desire may be present but there is likely not enough data points to draw conclusions. When Water@Work only had a handful of communities operating or in the process, it would have been difficult or nearly impossible to obtain the data we now collect. Even if it had been possible, a minimal number of data points are generally never enough to provide meaningful analysis.

With organizational experience comes the wisdom to understand critical areas and to draw the conclusions that lead to changes in the model. In most cases, the closer one gets to their customer, the more questions that are asked; and the more documentation that is received, the better one can provide effective accountability. This is one of the few expectations we have for our hub and distribution site customers—that they regularly participate in our effort to gather specific data. Of course while Water@Work continues to measure every possible activity to ensure positive results, a great many simply cannot or should not be formally measured.

On one side, we have manufacturing guru and statistician W. Edwards Deming stating emphatically:

"In God we trust, but all others must bring data."

And on the other, we have Albert Einstein with a sign on his office wall that stated:

> "Not everything that counts can be counted; and not everything that can be counted counts."

Water@Work certainly struggled with this. There was no argument in the merits of measuring performance in the areas of overall program success and individual critical areas, but we didn't want to hinder responsiveness and create bureaucracy. We settled in with evaluating each activity on the value/cost relationship of the effort. We were careful to employ relatively simple metrics that did not go so overboard as to become onerous. For this discussion we will examine the two applicable areas of activities within Water@Work: the DR-based operations and US-based operations.

DR-Based Operational Accountability

In a previous Chapter we were introduced to some of the terrific people that comprise our in-country team. They are primarily local folks that found their way into the organization through the construction process or by introduction from partners. Juan Luis Vilorio is one such young person that has grown in responsibility to now lead our in-country team.

Juan Luis was a vulnerable youth with a lot of promise – essentially the poster child for a great majority of the young men in the country. Without a stable job, he drifted around trying to find his place. While never getting into serious trouble, trouble always seemed to be just one bad decision away. Because he was the son of a pastor at a rural community church, he was very mature in his walk with Christ and never shies to voice his commitment to God. From our perspective, the proverbial diamond in the rough.

Like many others, he started working with Water@Work on constructing water plants. His potential quickly showed through, and he assumed a greater number and diversity of responsibilities. He honed his English skills incredibly quickly and ultimately settled into the role of community accountability liaison.

This is a critical role where he and other teammates would regularly go door to door in the communities and talk with customers on their satisfaction. At the same time, he would gather data on a great number of things that provided direct feedback on our successes or failings, as well as pray with the residents and share their concerns. The regularity of our presence in the community through Juan Luis and others had a major impact on the community accepting our efforts and help in their development efforts.

One doesn't have to be better at anything than everybody else. One only has to believe they can be better than they ever imagined through the power of the Spirit.

Juan Luis excelled in this role because he himself grew up in a poor rural community not much different from those we serve. He relates to our customers in ways that really help them and us. Because of his concern and skills, he always has a finger on the pulse of a particular community and can provide excellent feedback.

While Juan Luis would focus on community relations, technology compliance fell upon Alejandro Sheppard. Alejandro is a mature gentle man that worked odd jobs, primarily driving trucks whenever he could. He has a huge heart for God and regularly witnesses to many people. He also has lived with a pastor for an extended time in his life and is very educated in the Bible.

It is Alejandro's job to visit every Hub Site and test the water for quality assurance. He has a regular route that takes him to every site on average one per month. Water@Work utilizes a quick water quality test that detects any bacteria in the water after only eighteen hours. It further does this without any special treatment of the water such as controlling temperature or light sensitivity. This quick test enables the team to provide significant quality control of the water produced at less than pennies per test.

In addition, the water is taken to our formal testing laboratory located at the Water@Work headquarters once every month. There, it undergoes more extensive testing with environmental controls to verify that the water exceeds government requirements.

While on site, Alejandro will also check the equipment to ensure everything is working properly and no repairs are needed. Regular maintenance of the equipment is very important for its longevity, and Alejandro sees that any filters or membranes that need replacing or cleaning get done immediately.

While Juan Luis leads the in-country support team and Alejandro assists, others further contribute and are being trained to take over the leadership opportunities that will present themselves as an ever greater number of Hub Sites are built in the future. They also assist in conducting regular site and customer surveys that provide very valuable information. Consistently having "feet on the ground" and regular visits by the same people also enables helpful observational analysis. Change is easier to identify and local residents open up more easily when they regularly see the same staff supporting them. However, for as important as the information is, the sheer size and makeup of the country often present a significant logistical challenge.

The Dominican Republic is a surprisingly large country that shares the island of Hispaniola with its smaller neighbor, Haiti. According to the US State Department, the country's land mass has been compared to the state of South Carolina or the combination of Vermont and New Hampshire. Whether this is accurate or not, anyone that has attempted to cross the country will tell you it takes about two days to do so. Unfortunately, there is a mountain that rises over 10,000 feet in elevation near the center of the country and a very sparse road network. Coupled with the reality that many bateys are not located near paved or easily accessible roads and regular visits are a necessity, accessibility is indeed challenging.

US-Based Operational Accountability

Water@Work took a huge risk in bringing on its first intern at a time when we really didn't know what to do or expect. One day a young man named Gary Jones contacted us through our website. He was close to graduating from the University of Arizona with a degree in Environmental Science, and was looking for ways to help after graduation. At first, we decided to pass because we thought we weren't ready. Over time and many discussions going back and forth on the risks and potential benefits, God seemed to want to make it happen. So it did.

Gary soon moved to the Dominican and agreed to three months of service supporting our team in-country. When those three months ended, he decided to stay on an additional month and a half to finish up some of his project work. That was it. The inexplicable vortex of serving in these communities sucked him up and he wanted to make his missionary service a full time commitment. There was only one little problem...

Back home in Arizona he had a serious girlfriend that he wanted to be with as well - as in permanently. So when Gary finally returned home, he married Paty. After a short engagement, they prayed diligently on what path their new life together should take. We could not have been more excited when Gary decided to come on board as our Sustainability Coordinator. It is a critical role that he and his skill set are perfect for.

As the US based Sustainability Coordinator, about one third of his time is in the Dominican Republic and two thirds are at home in Arizona. His primary responsibility is to collect and aggregate data to measure progress in particular communities and success against the parameters set by the organization. He is a central point of contact and is fluent in the culture and language. We are able to rely on him to keep us informed of operational challenges, opportunities and progress.

Gary made some really difficult decisions for a young man in a very short time. In less than two years, he passed on a stateside career in environmental science and the financial stability that goes with it, moved to another country without the benefit of a program to fit into, came back to get married, and decided to work full time for our non-profit. Whew!

His position ensures that we always have continuity between our domestic and international operations. The stateside team maintains accountability through a number of procedures and people. By working in a team environment most decisions become thoroughly vetted. In the Dominican, the team maintains accountability by regular visits to our customer communities and cross-training of individuals.

Gary is a link between those two different worlds and operations, providing our Board and management team with great visibility into the progress of any particular project, thus enabling good accountability for them and our donor customers.

However, it would be misleading to make this appear as if we have it all figured out. Gary is "flying blind" in that just about everything he does is a first for us. He is not immune from the struggle this creates:

> *"Somehow God has given me the strength to not get too discouraged or to give up. I feel like all of the challenges have helped, though. Now as challenges come, it almost feels normal. That doesn't mean that I don't have a hard time still, but I know it will be OK."*

With the benefit of youth and its deep reservoir of energy, as well as a firm reliance on God, he is overcoming obstacles to make a huge difference. He also prays diligently about his next major decision: to move in-country and become full time missionaries with Paty. As God would make it, Paty is originally from Venezuela, a preacher's kid, and speaks fluent Spanish. Gary's dream is to move together, with him focused on the water side and she focused on evangelism. At times as an older person you look at a young couple and realize they are going to have a great life together. Gary and Paty will be just fine serving Christ and riding the wave.

As we have seen, accountability is extremely important to ensure organizational efficiency, sound communications and continuous improvement. This is a very important inward perspective that serves both the organization and its customers. But I have yet to meet any organization that can operate effectively and still "go it alone". As we'll see in the next few chapters, partnerships are incredibly important.

Life Lesson 14

Taking calculated chances after prayerful discernment can lead to decisions that may forever change your life.

From Gary to you:

You will keep in perfect peace him whose mind is steadfast, because he trusts in you.
Isaiah 26:3 (NIV)

I love this verse. I know that peace only comes through the Lord. We have to trust that God will provide, calm the storm, redeem and take care of us. It's hard at times and I'm always learning!

Living in the Dominican required learning another culture and language, which has its challenges, but I'm thankful for what I have learned from them. It so easy to think our American way is better than theirs. Sometimes it is, but many times it isn't. I've learned so much from them and how they live.

Honestly, I kind of like that my job has changed a lot. It keeps things interesting! I don't feel like I have been creating the job but more just figuring out how I fit into the ministry and helping where I'm needed. Paty has been a huge help and has supported me so much during all of these transitions, and is learning where she fits into the ministry as well. I'm thankful that we can encourage one another and seek the Lord together.

15. In-Country Partners

> *"Two are better than one, because they have a good reward for their toil. For if they fall, one will lift up his fellow. But woe to him who is alone when he falls and has not another to lift him up! ... And though a man might prevail against one who is alone, two will withstand him—a threefold cord is not quickly broken."*
>
> *Ecclesiastes 4:9-12*

Partnerships can be tough. They hold tremendous promise, yet require different resources and skills to fully exploit the potential benefits. Like it or not, , the need to find effective partners to expand the capacity of a non-profit is essential in the maturing of a non-profit organization. The Amherst H. Wilder Foundation conducted a Study in the year 2000 that correctly frames the issue:

> *"Many small, community-based groups are organizationally fragile. Many large groups are stretched to their limits. As demand for community-based services grows, as new needs are identified, and as new paradigms for exchange and interaction emerge, the non-profit sector is continually challenged to devise ways to increase and strengthen its capacity. Indeed, capacity building must rest on the notion that change is the norm."*

Every organization, for profit and not for profit, struggles with cost effective capacity building. Partnering in the for-profit sector is generally limited by factors that address the need to maintain proprietary information and a general desire to "sell what one knows." For-profits more readily embrace retaining temporary employees or hiring contractors and contract organizations to provide a function they may not be able to fulfil with their current staff and resources (organizational capacity).

Their desire to partner with other organizations is typically driven by trying to gain access to other markets or provide a significant resource that it cannot cost-effectively supply on its own. The rarity of for-profit partnering speaks to the difficulties inherent in the venture. The luxury that for-profits enjoy is the financial resources to obtain those capabilities it desires through hiring and other financially expeditious means. If it will produce a greater profit, the means to achieve it can generally be justified and procured.

This is very different from the non-profit sector. Here, the financial resources rarely exist to hire on a particular skill set. As we have seen and discussed previously, donors expect their gift to be utilized in providing a service to a community and not for the acquisition of organizational capacity. As such, non-profits are increasingly being required to build partnerships to increase capacity.

In an earlier chapter, we saw how growth is achieved primarily through working things out with people of differing mindsets, as opposed to those of the same ilk which often reflects the comfortable choice. A similar perspective is true for trust development among potential partners in a faraway geography or international ministry. With distance comes unfamiliarity. The very essence of a partnership is trust, and trust can generally only be gained by nurturing familiarity through time together. Unfortunately, the one thing a fledgling international ministry does not generally have is enough time in-country to develop trusting partnerships where they could be beneficial. It is simply too expensive to travel and invest such precious time.

Even mature non-profit organizations have issues in developing effective partnerships. Any organization worth its salt will try and hire local people to conduct its services in foreign countries. While this is laudable and practiced by Water@Work as well, the local personnel seldom feel empowered to develop partnerships. Please forgive me for being politically sensitive there. The harsh reality is that most international staff does not have enough quality time with their US-based counterparts to feel true authority or empowerment.

The most educated and experienced people, as well as the money, come from America. The unfortunate norm is that local representatives will generally not make any move, or even suggest a move, that has a chance to be viewed negatively back in America.

Culture even works against us here. You may have heard of island time. I assure you it actually exists, and it is the exact opposite of American culture. Island time regularly manifests itself in daily life. It is all too common to schedule a meeting for 10:00 and the locals show up, maybe, around 10:45. But it also exists emotionally, such as how it is totally out of character for a Dominican to question you. They seem to avoid any conflict, particularly with those that can potentially make their life better. It's truly enough to drive a driven American crazy.

This reality is not just apropos to the Dominican Republic. The relaxed nature of life pretty much everywhere outside the United States makes trust-building and partnerships even more difficult because our culture appears aggressive to them. That perception is many times at the core of difficult, trust developing conversations.

The benefit that Christian based organizations have here is that often trust is expected and easily built because of the commonality of Christ. A Christian in the Dominican Republic understands the concept and scriptures about the Body of Christ. They understand that we are all small but integral parts of the Body that have been instructed to work together by our Lord. True enough, and we rely on this all the time, but it can still be frustratingly difficult.

Necessity is the Mother of all Partnership

Whenever one enters into partnership, whether with an individual or organization, both parties have expectations of both conduct and performance. Value must be received and provided in relative equality for there to be a long term successful relationship. It is in this vein that our first organizational partnership formed.

Bishop Cancu is the leader of the Evangelical Church of the Dominican Republic, also referred to the IED. He is a towering figure with a gentle, soft and meek voice. That is until he is asked to give a prayer. Then like an approaching freight train, he starts slow and builds to where one fears the walls will fall. When he invites Christ into a meeting, you become absolutely certain Christ is there!

He is also a frustrated leader. He has a vision for his church to be spiritually vibrant, financially stable, and a true resource to the poor. Its rich history started over a century ago when the Methodist Church, Presbyterian Church and Monrovian Church came together to found it. Over this time it has grown into the largest protestant denomination in the country. But because the church operates in primarily the very poor parts of the country, including the bateys, it is continually struggling for funds.

Poor in this case actually means poor by Dominican standards. I was blessed to once attend a typical service in a batey at a small church with perhaps fifty persons attending. After the collection plate was passed around and the service was over, I was shocked to see three coins in the plate rendering a total giving of approximately $0.75! On any given Sunday, nearly one-third of the pastors in the congregation will go without any salary. If they are fortunate enough, they have full time jobs working in the fields next to their congregants. If not, they get by like the majority of the flock they serve.

The poverty they deal with financially is in stark contrast to the spiritual abundance shown down on them by the Holy Spirit. Their worship services are typically very uplifting and joyful, filled with much singing and congregant involvement. This seemed like the perfect organization for us to partner with. They already had a relationship with John, our in-country coordinator, they needed stable financial resources that could come from selling the clean water, the communities they served were aching for development, and their leader, Bishop Cancu, totally understood and embraced the vision. While we would still install water plants with other denominations, we would build them at the IED sites whenever our donors did not specify a particular location or denomination.

Since first partnering with them, the benefits have truly gone both ways in spades. From their perspective the water plants have brought in a significant windfall of funds to build improved church facilities, badly needed schools, and a host of other important community projects. Importantly, the church has been seen as the catalyst for change. It was the church that brought the community good health, extra family income, and the social programs so desperately needed. With this positive exposure and relevance in their lives, more and more villagers started to attend church. Baptisms and conversions blossomed, and the communities prospered from the myriad of benefits we have discussed.

From our perspective, we received what we needed most—a trusted voice to help us understand the culture and introductions to other synergistic organizations, as well as an interface with the government. Over time their honest feedback became critical to the development of our model.

A Notable Failure

In the early days, we were evaluating a different model for financing the in-country support team that involved a micro-business approach. Micro-business non-profits typically provide very small loans for individuals looking to start a small business. A great example is the large number of people at the street corners of major international cities that sell everything imaginable. Windshield wipers, cell phone charges, bottles of water, fruit, nuts, and pretty much what anyone could need is available.

However, in order to start these "small businesses" the individual needs between a few dollars and a few hundred dollars for inventory. There are several excellent non-profit organizations step in and provide the loan to people with nearly zero credit worthiness.

We partnered with one such non-profit because we loved their commitment to evangelism through their operations. As an example, they would have weekly meetings with all their loan recipients to review their financials, then accept and record a small amount for loan repayment. They would take advantage of these meetings to also require a Bible Study at the same time. A meeting that might last half an hour could now run a couple hours as their personnel led their customers in discipleship growth.

This seemed like a terrific organization for us to partner with. We certainly shared the same values and motivations, and the micro-finance seemed a like a reasonable fit. We worked for many months with their in-country Executive Director, a committed Dominican brother in Christ and their local representative to work out a possible relationship. Unfortunately, the cost of our water plants was far greater than the loan amounts that comfortably fit into their existing model and working together seemed a stretch.

It was at this point that we experienced a perfect example of the lack of empowerment by in-country personnel funded by American non-profits. The in-country Executive Director communicated with his American Board of Directors and the idea of a partnership was quickly rejected. Though he had worked many months to develop a model modification that he felt would have worked, the Americans that were responsible for his funding didn't see the vision. I certainly understand their perspective. We were stretching their model significantly and they didn't feel they had the revenues to fund the greater cost. In hindsight, it is fairly clear the partnership would not have worked.

The point here is not that they rejected the partnership, as that was undoubtedly a very good decision based upon their funding realities and model. Rather, the point is how the culture succeeded in having us both spend a lot of time on an effort that was essentially a no-go from the start.

The in-country Executive Director worked many months vetting our prospective partnership, and felt his in-country organization could handle the new opportunity. However, in his heart he knew it would be a tough sell back in America. After many months, he finally approached his Board and the partnership was vetoed in a heartbeat.

Incredible amounts of time and energy were flushed with a single pull. This is unfortunately an all too typical experience of a "disconnect" between in-country and American management based on cultural perspectives and empowerment. We parted ways pledging to support each other's organizations and efforts with regular prayer support.

The Foundation for Peace Partnership

Another early partner that came forward was the Foundation for Peace and their in-country leader, an American missionary by the name of Kristin Hamner. This was our first partnership where an exchange of value could be measured, and exemplifies why in-country partnerships can yield a terrific return on one's time and effort.

The Foundation brings about 650 volunteers each year to the Dominican Republic. They have served in more than fifty communities, including a dozen bateys, and are totally committed to assisting these communities in their development. The Foundation selects their communities based on the potential of the pastor located there, as well as where their impact can be significant. Sharing similar beliefs and strategies as us, the partnership flourished.

Kristin is a rare type that doesn't easily fit most categories. Raised in a loving Christian family from rural Nebraska and living in the Dominican most of her adult life as a missionary, she exhibits a special passion that is infectious. When she sets her mind to something, it is generally best to get out of the way. Her relentless work ethic truly stands out, as exemplified by the achievement of a Master's Degree in Divinity while still building the in-country operations of the Foundation.

She has also been able to successfully walk the fine line between being American and "going island." She is equally adept at negotiating with the local businesses in their dialect, or providing logistics for the dozens of short term missionary teams from America that she hosts every year.

We still lovingly laugh at the time when Kristin wanted to celebrate a long week of hard work. We were elated when she offered dinner at a local restaurant on the beach. This is likely not the beautiful, scenic vision you have in mind. It was a crowded row of tents and shacks with local people either milling around or cooking lobster and other fish caught that day. It was the kind of place that makes your instincts say no, but the smells from dozens of open fires grilling seafood makes you go for it.

While Kristin was negotiating with one particular cook she knew, I tipped a person a few dollars to get a table with a nice view. You would have thought someone had stolen our last dollar. She let loose on this poor soul in double-barrel flawless Spanish. How dare he take money from a missionary for a table that we should have just been given! Everyone there became certain we had a special person that would look out for us and our interests. We also had one of the better meals that I can ever remember.

Kristin became a vital early set of eyes for us, identifying and providing information on specific bateys that we needed to be successful. In return, we supplied a water plant that provided the clean water and development funds so desperately needed to the communities the Foundation served. This is a perfect illustration of a very typical and successful foreign country quid pro quo.

The Foundation also regularly shipped large amounts of donated goods to the island. They further helped us by providing essentially free shipping to Santo Domingo, as well as warehouse space to store the equipment. One of the seriously difficult situations involved with an international ministry is import fees, tariffs, taxes and, in some parts of the world, serious graft among the customs officials and dock workers. The Foundation had worked through all those issues and being able to get equipment in the country painlessly was a tremendous value.

Interestingly, Kristin sought us out. It was the first indication of how aggressively she looked for ways to improve the communities they served. I don't think there is anything, short of illegalities, that she wouldn't do for her communities. She and her team are powerful advocates for the poor, and we were gratefully schooled in the nuances of getting things done.

The Government as a Partner

The government in most foreign lands is anything but a partner. Graft, theft, deceit and antagonism are more the norm than healthy relations based on mutual respect and true partnership. The Dominican was different for us. While the levels of bureaucracy and the number of hoops required to jump through are staggering, we eventually found some great people to work with that have yielded significant benefits.

As we built an increasing number of water plants across the country, we started to get the attention of the government. We decided to be proactive and meet with the Public Health Department for the country. Initially, we were petrified. We had heard many stories. However, after many months of meetings and developing a level of trust, we were honored to meet with Senior Nunez, the Assistant Director of the Department.

During these discussions he tested our sincerity by requiring us to significantly enhance our water plants. While they loved our E-RO technology, they required many upgrades to the physical building itself. While many of these seemed usurious, we agreed to everything they asked. An old sales tenet is that the easiest way to get to a "yes" is to eliminate all the possible reasons to say "no." Ultimately, after even more meetings he uttered what we longed to hear:

"How can we help?"

Wow. *How can we help?* Let me count the ways! While we would have been happy to just have the government not be in our way, they actually became a great partner that we gratefully had in our camp. They became proud to state that there was finally a missionary group in their country that was building "legal" water plants. We were just overjoyed to know that our communities could operate and sell their water without fear of the government shutting down their operations.

Of course as often happens with government, people change with administrations and we eventually lost Senor Nunez. Even though we lost the individual, the core of the relationship continues to remain healthy.

Equally important to external or in-country partners is a strong network of partners back home. In our next chapter we will meet some of these organizations and individuals that facilitate the growth of our management and fund raising efforts.

Life Lesson 15
It is worth the effort to develop partnerships in-country when the foundation is service to Christ. It is equally difficult to imagine how true partnerships can flourish outside this commonality.

From Kristin to you:

I am so glad to be part of the chapter on partnership - because partnerships are the way both of our organizations roll. Like Water@Work, the Foundation for Peace is constantly seeking out both local community partners and global partners to energize our efforts. We like to say, 'we can't do everything, but we are willing to do anything.'

Due to the desperate need for water in our communities, I was eager to learn about Water@Work. I had met a number of groups who were installing water systems, and most were (in my opinion) making mistakes that prevented their results from matching their good intentions. So I approached Water@Work with excitement, but also wariness.

I was delighted to find an organization that was willing to listen to the needs of the local communities. Most come in-country with a standard delivery model and the arrogance to think that their model was the right one for every community and situation. They were willing to adapt their model to fit local requirements.

I look forward to a long and mutually beneficial relationship to the glory of God and for the benefit of the Dominican and Haitian people we both serve.

16. Home~Based Partners

> *"And he gave the apostles, the prophets, the evangelists, the shepherds and teachers, to equip the saints for the work of ministry, for building up the body of Christ,"*
>
> *Ephesians 4:11-12*

As important as it is to have great partnerships in the country of operations, so it is in the home country as well. In a differing capacity, however, partners at home tend to be in the vein of raising resources, awareness and funds. Here is where domestic non-profits have the upper hand over international non-profits like Water@Work. The reasons for this are three-fold:

1. Domestic ministry efforts are local. Because all operations and community exposure is local, many people will see the efforts of the organization in the community and respond. Awareness of the mission becomes much more difficult when the service provided by the non-profit is in a different country.

2. Familiarity breeds empathy. Most people in the United States can place themselves in the aftermath of a tornado, hurricane, or snow storm. Similarly, most can sympathize with homelessness, childhood illnesses, disease research, or any of the thousands of civic and philanthropic opportunities to help. It is significantly more difficult to establish familiarity with children getting sick and dying from contaminated water—a situation that America eliminated as a threat over a hundred years ago.

3. Foreign cultures just seem so *foreign*. It is very hard to relate to life in the bateys and ultra-poor rural communities of the Dominican Republic. With conditions that can best be compared

to indentured servitude, few Americans can fully relate to the lives of people there that live in pure survival mode.

Whether international or domestic, every non-profit must establish strong partnerships with their constituents and donors to achieve their mission. In many cases, the partnership may be more of a significant relationship than a formal documented partnership, but these are the associations that enable the organization to ultimately sink or swim.

To be clear, we are not talking about internal personnel and advisors. The key to a healthy non-profit is the exceptional people that live and breathe the mission, as well as individuals that serve in professional capacities such as on a Board of Directors or Advisory Board. The relationships we will explore here are with people or organizations that can significantly further a mission with expert input, donations or passionate fervor.

You may be that someone and not fully realize it. Are you a person that actually understands the tax code and can keep everything legal? Perhaps you can move a conversation from virtually any subject to a cause near your heart and never miss a beat. Or maybe you are creative in problem solving and human relations. If you are of that type person, then you are indeed fortunate because God has blessed you in ways beyond measure.

If you are not actively involved in a ministry and using your skills or passion then you have the terrific opportunity to be a significant partner to some ministry somewhere. I cannot imagine *not* being involved in something much bigger than me or my personal problems. In a social setting I need to be corralled by my family and friends so as to not talk incessantly about Water@Work. Because God called me to it, it's the most important thing in my life and I feel a need to share it. Yeah, I'm one of those guys.

Is That Really Jack the Baptist?

Another one of those guys is Jack Weymiller. I met Jack on my first mission trip to the Dominican, the one that got this whole thing moving in the first place. He was introduced to me as Jack the Baptist and spoken of in very high regard by everyone at the mission house. As it turned out, back in the Atlanta area he lived within a half hour of me and we met in fellowship regularly.

After a few years, I realized that while Jack the Baptist was really a great guy, I hardly saw him as responsible for exceptional numbers of baptisms. It was then he "fessed up" and told me that he was the only Baptist in Rivers of the World (ROW), a non-profit heavily connected with the Presbyterian denomination. Jack the Baptist was just an easy way for everyone to distinguish him from a couple other Jacks involved in their non-profit. It was a bit playfully disingenuous, but worthy of a good belly laugh nonetheless.

Putting titles aside, Jack fully grasped the vision we had for the Dominican and began spreading the word. Having successfully been in professional sales much of his life, Jack went forward and consistently secured funding for several water plants every year. Even better, because ROW's primary mission was to lead short term mission trips to many locations around the world, including the Dominican Republic, his efforts provided a double benefit. Not only were the required funds for the entire program secured, but he also provided construction teams from his churches that helped build the physical water plant and thereby lowered the total cost further.

As his job was to introduce American churches to the bateys we both served, our partnership was truly made in heaven. But what really helped was his grasp of "professional sales." There is unfortunately a stigma in non-profits against the use of the word sales. The word seems to imply a dirtiness or ugliness that is truly regrettable. There seems to be a prevailing notion that selling something must result in one party taking advantage of another party.

Professional sales are all about the opposite. A professional salesperson would not try to force someone into a relationship that did not result in a mutual win. It's all about understanding what one has to offer, pairing that with people that could benefit from it, and doing so to produce mutual value or gain. It's a matter of good business vs. bad business. Bad business results in a short term sale or gain, but ultimately costs more. Professional salespersons that are committed to Christ clearly understand this, and can be a huge asset to a non-profit.

Never underestimate the impact of an individual. Because of this partnership and Jack's personal efforts, those water plants are providing safe drinking water for many tens of thousands that would otherwise go without. But not all partnerships necessarily lead to donations. Some, like the one we will explore next, involve some nurturing.

A Square Peg in a Sea of Round Holes

It's not always about money. I met Joe Burns completely by "accident" at his local church. I was asked to demonstrate our technology for someone else and the easiest place was at his church. While we were discussing the technology, Joe walked by and immediately realized the benefits of the technology.

Joe has a very interesting career as a helicopter pilot. He worked for one of the local Atlanta news channels ferrying reporters around town to get the "just breaking" stories. Perhaps pretty glamorous, but flying for many hours to sometimes dangerous locations and in hazardous conditions was brutal on the body. More importantly, Joe shared with me his longing to be involved in a ministry where he could contribute a significant impact for the kingdom.

A helicopter pilot? That's a tough one. We agreed to pray on his future and were sure that after making it clear to God that he was ready to more fully utilize his gifts for His service, God would open the appropriate door. Pretty much nothing happened for a while.

We couldn't figure out the value of a helicopter pilot to our budding ministry, and his work schedule was absolutely crazy.

Prayer is a great start, middle, and finish to anything. But God also expects us to take concrete steps forward in faith.

So while faithfully praying for guidance, Joe took a huge step towards God. Realizing that his schedule was precluding him from the type of active ministry he longed to be a part of, he changed jobs. He left the near insanity of network news coverage and took on a terrific position as a helicopter pilot for a local children's hospital. The best thing about the change was that he would now work seven days on and seven days off, providing days' worth of free time to actively serve.

God in His greatness knew that putting Joe into a great ministry while subject to significant impediments like he was experiencing would end in failure and frustration. Like many of us, Joe was praying for a direct and immediate solution to his dilemma. God instead chose to bring Joe along in steps that ultimately led him to Water@Work and a situation more conducive to serving the kingdom.

That's also when we learned of Joe's quietly overlooked true skill set. We saw Joe as a great helicopter pilot, full of courage and precise skills. What we learned over time was that the real strength of Joe lay in his incredible capacity for deep prayer and spiritual relationships. Through the difficult months and years of searching, we knew Joe would be great serving God through Water@Work first in church relations and then ultimately as a leader in our evangelism efforts.

We initially focused on Joe's career skills, but then came to see him for where his true gifts lay. I think this is true in many instances. When looking at someone that has an interest in serving a non-profit, often the process is about what they do for a living or what type of education they have. Joe's experience really reinforced for us that it should rarely be about someone's resume. We couldn't find a good fit with a helicopter pilot, but we found a great fit with a person of passion and desire to serve.

So while we have looked at a how we work with another ministry and individuals like Joe, a third very important type of partnership here in America is our relationships with churches.

Church Partnerships

Churches in the United States account for an exceptionally large percentage of the giving to non-profits. When it comes to international non-profits, the percentage is even higher. I cannot over-emphasize the importance of our church partners. They "get" our ministry like no other group. And they are typically frustrated by decades of giving with little to show for it.

While there have thankfully been untold numbers of persons saved to an eternity with our Lord, the greatest return on investment ever, no other group has experienced the lack of development in the developing world as they. Certainly there are many governmental and non-governmental organizations measuring the issues and making many laudable strides, but none *feel* it like the churches.

Having traveled to the Dominican Republic many, many times, I have been in and out of the Santo Domingo airport more times than I can remember. The one thing that strikes you after a number of times is the number of short term missionaries coming and going. Everywhere one looks you see people of all ages with matching mission shirts from one American church or another. These short term missions, coupled with long term missionaries financially supported by the churches, are the true agents of change in the developing world.

While these visits are great for the communities they serve, I don't think many would argue that the real beneficiaries of these trips are the missionaries themselves. The vast majority come home changed to the core and hungry to plug in somewhere and continue the impact that they felt while in-country. Certainly I was in this camp and it was a short term mission trip like this that ultimately led to Water@Work.

The work done in these trips truly spreads Christ's love, and the actual work performed by the team also certainly has direct benefits to the people being served. Unfortunately, most of the efforts expended result in temporary benefits.

- Building latrines? They will eventually fill and need to be re-built elsewhere.

- Providing medical help? With the exception of surgical procedures that remove some disabling or limiting feature, people will get sick again.

- Providing VBS? After one leaves, when is the next time the children will have exposure to the good news again?

You get the idea, but please don't go to burn this book just yet. There are certainly many long term benefits to whatever mission work your team is doing. Most importantly, the long term value by local residents from exposure to a mission team just spreading the gospel through the love they share is immeasurable.

My point is more towards questions such as:

- How many activities will still be fully effective three to four generations from now?

- How many activities will lead to sustaining job development?

- How many activities will empower the local church to effectively evangelize to the unreached in their community for many years?

- How many activities will support and nurture the development of community leaders?

- How many activities will bring great health to entire communities for many, many decades?

- How many activities will lead to the development of commerce in the communities?

One of the reasons I believe that Water@Work has been so successful with its church partners is because churches are hungry to move from the temporary to lasting. Of critical importance is that lasting change can still occur while all the temporary benefits continue to be experienced by both the short term missionaries and in-country community residents. We can have the heavenly cake and eat it too.

Another reason churches are our best partners is because many are looking for construction opportunities for their mission teams. Building our water plants and distribution sites at local Dominican churches makes for perfect week-long mission projects.

Lastly, many churches rightly promote giving by their congregations specifically for international mission work and are looking for ministries like ours to assist with donations. We are beyond grateful to the churches that review our ministry activities and decide to help us financially. While we have partnered with many different Christian denominations, one specific example is the United Methodist Church (UMC). Water@Work is humbled that the UMC has accepted the Water@Work ministry into their Advance Program. Being in the Advance Program has led to many great relationships with UMC churches of all sizes that send construction teams down to the Dominican, provide mentoring and financial donations.

Life Lesson 16

Nurturing ministry or non-profit based relationships and partnerships, whether in or out of country, take far more effort than traditional business and, in many cases, more than personal relationships.

From Joe to you:

One of the great surprises of working in mission is how God may use the unexpected to move you into new territory. This happened to me when I was asked to facilitate a Water@Work Evangelism and Best Practices Summit in the DR. Despite our exhaustive preparations, the event went off into areas we could never have dreamed of. The highlight was an impromptu game of baseball played with a stick and ball made from crushed paper. Baseball seems to be everything in the DR. The Bishop participated and God used the fun to bring everyone together and truly open up in some incredible ways.

It is just one example of the terrific experiences one can only gain from being involved in any aspect of ministry. My advice to anyone reading this is to just get involved and enjoy where God puts you and how He uses you. Never mind the effort, He seems to love on-the-job training!

Part 4

Can Ministry Really Change Anything?

17. Stories from the Front Lines

"He told them, "The harvest is plentiful, but the workers are few. Ask the Lord of the harvest, therefore, to send out workers into his harvestfield."

Luke 10:2

Now it's time to take a deeper and more in-depth look at some of the very personal stories of people that are the heart and soul of Water@Work. These are stories from ordinary folks that through varying levels of involvement use their personal gifts to share the love of Christ. It will focus on their thoughts and perspectives prior to and after making the decision to follow God's leading voice into various levels of ministry involvement.

"The idea that service to God should have only to do with a church alter, singing, reading, sacrifice, and the like is without doubt but the worst trick of the devil. How could the devil have led us more effectively astray than by the narrow conception that the service of God takes place only in the church and by works done therein. ... The whole world could abound with services to the Lord... not only in churches but also in the home, kitchen, workshop, and field."

- Martin Luther

This book has endeavored to tell the story of Water@Work through the voices of those that serve her. Sometimes that service is manifested through direct hours spent on committee or operational function of the ministry. Many times, however, we see important involvement that plays out in private acts of worship that often go

165

"unnoticed" by human eyes. The following are stories from both camps that may further illuminate the impact felt through all types and levels of involvement

Donna Bearden, a Nurse

Donna visited her first batey in 2001 while a part of a medical mission team from Statesboro, Georgia, and it changed her life. One day, a mother entered the batey clinic carrying her limp child in her arms. As she gently placed the frail child, nearly depleted of life from a high fever, infection, and dehydration in a chair, the child could barely support herself. After a few minutes, Donna noticed the child begin to heave as if she needed to vomit. As the child began to choke, Donna was horrified to see a live worm coming from the side of the child's mouth. The child continued to heave and eventually vomited a handful of live worms on the floor.

This was Donna's pivotal moment of when He called her loudly.

The mortality rate of the children in the batey was a staggering 50% due to parasitic infections, primarily from contaminated water. The only source of drinking water in the batey was an irrigation ditch where much of the human and animal fecal matter from the community drained. Donna decided then and there to devote her skills to resolving the problem at its source. Instead of treating symptoms, she was determined to bring clean drinking water to this and other communities in need.

For years, Donna was haunted by that little girl and the many others she came to know. She felt a call to become a missionary and work full time on her new passion, but the timing was always difficult. With two girls between the ages of nine and sixteen, a husband midway through his career, and her responsibilities at a local hospital, it seemed there would be no way to make it happen. She describes herself at that time as a typical materialistic person, always wanting the best for her and her family and never having enough time in the day.

Then, like Erv Kimble whom we met in Chapter One, she did an unexpected thing and made her part-time passion into a full-time ministry. With the spiritual and financial support of a terrific church family and the loving support of her husband and children, they all moved to the Dominican Republic. Donna continued to serve as a nurse in places that rarely saw medical help and never relented in her quest for sustainable clean community water. Her husband John supported local Dominican churches that struggled in their management and leadership of the many US church mission teams that regularly visited.

For many years they did just that, as well as home school the children, learn the language, the culture, and build up huge doses of patience. The satisfaction of acquiring "things" turned to the joy of a much simpler life dedicated to serving those in need. While in America, Donna didn't see herself as prideful, yet the lifestyle of living in a foreign land humbled her in unmeasurable ways. Living as the poor people they served drew their family much closer. For some time, support and encouragement only came from each other.

Donna and Water@Work met after they had been on the island for several very difficult years. While the family grew to love the people, they still struggled with their place amongst a culture so foreign. Over time, she learned a critical truism that has value for those of us here as well. She has discovered real happiness from their absolute reliance on God for all provisions and safety, and in the relationships with many "neighbors" that society seems to pass by. Her foreign life and lifestyle started to make sense when she focused on the people and not the task. True success is measured in the number of souls touched and not in the accumulation of things or jobs well done. Ouch. Now that's a tough one for most Americans.

For years I would travel to the Dominican working on the origins of Water@Work and I would hear about Donna. Everyone said we needed to meet, but it never worked out. Her family would actually joke and refer to me as the Water Oz, as in the man behind the curtain from the Wizard of Oz that nobody ever met, but with a water obsession. Our team actually wondered the same thing about the mythical nurse named Donna.

It was one of those "God" moments when Water@Work and Donna connected. The fit was perfect and she became Evangelism Team leader. Her focus is supporting community pastors with a Water@Work plant to utilize the clean water in spreading the Gospel in the region. She also works at developing relationships between United States churches and local Dominican pastors for evangelism development. Leveraging clean water for evangelism is her passion, but her medical bag is of course never far away.

When asked if being involved in ministry has changed her relationship with Christ, she clearly and simply says:

> *"Absolutely. I now know more than ever that what the Bible says is true … God is near to the broken hearted and suffering. I consider myself blessed to see His heavenly handiwork every day."*

Dan Blevins, a Retired Chemist

As the year came to an end in 2011, all of us at Water@Work were frustrated by in-country coordination and management concerns. Water plant construction in the Dominican had slowed terribly, and we were having a host of challenges at local sites awaiting installation. As I was the one at Water@Work responsible for their progress, I knew better than anyone that we needed serious help in a major way.

I prayed a very specific prayer that went along the lines of "Dear God, your ministry is growing faster than we can handle and I don't have the time to do a good job. We need someone with a scientific skill set that can devote nearly full time effort and be free to travel a lot. Oh yeah, we don't have any money for a salary, so it has to be someone that can work for free. Thanks." While I don't like to think we were quite as desperate as that may sound, it's reflective of our feelings at the time.

Literally before our team had its next meeting, I met Dan Blevins for lunch because a mutual friend thought we should know each other. This time our prayer was answered quickly! Actually, it was as literal an answer as one can imagine. Dan had retired from his life as a leader at Dow Chemical, working there his entire professional life as a chemist and project manager. Because he had a nice retirement pension and a still-working wife, is an eminently capable scientist, and is able to serve nearly full time, travel freely, and not require a salary, he was perfect! Thanks, God.

It's only appropriate that Dan was searching just like us. In the years leading up to his retirement, he prayerfully and actively sought opportunities to serve. He had very good health and was excited to use his retirement to give back a bit. For a few initial years he served his church in many capacities and traveled to Africa on multiple mission trips. Through these efforts he narrowed down his service desires to helping in the clean water crisis with an opportunity that maximized his life skills. He was essentially looking for just what we needed. Thanks again, God.

Dan has taken to the ministry and the hard work like a fish to water. Well, perhaps a salmon swimming upstream may be more accurate. The technical challenges of implementing very sophisticated water technology in a different country without reliable electricity and varying conditions of source water is rarely easy. Fortunately, Dan takes it all in stride and still manages to sing in his church's acclaimed choir.

Dan first served Water@Work on its Implementation Committee for about half a year. During that time he and we probed each other and sought to determine the character of the other. He also took the time to discern if this was his best fit, as he had always thought he would continue his work in Africa.

I would strongly urge anyone wanting to get involved as a volunteer in a non-profit to take their time like Dan did. Even if you have powerhouse credentials and are used to leadership, it can't be overstated that serving first in entry type activities is a great way to observe the organization in action. Organizations have a type of

DNA, and active low-exposure participation and observation will enable it to show through.

As the Director of Operations for Water@Work, Dan has grown to become arguably one of the most critical people in the organization. We would describe his job as simply to make the vision of the mission a reality. He personally describes it as "ensuring everything happens on schedule." Either way, he is critical to success. He accomplishes that by overseeing site selection, water plant construction, technology installations, and maintenance and community relations. He is a central figure to whom all in-country employees and volunteers report to. He is also the go-to guy for everyone here in home operations.

For all his travels to Africa and around the world, Dan was initially ignorant of the situation in the bateys and rural communities of the Dominican. He may have started out as a scientist, calculating everything in a detached, professional manner, but has since grown to fall in love with the people and children. His funniest memory of his service revolves around a group of children arguing that what they were calling a cockroach was, in actuality, a tarantula. Despite the tarantula being native to their country, they didn't have a name for it.

If we are fortunate, we will all face retirement at some point. With the aging of the baby boomer generation it seems library shelves overflow with tomes on achieving a rewarding retirement. But I think when Richard Bach, the accomplished author of *Johnathon Livingston Seagull*, succinctly wrote the following, he not only nailed it but could have been describing Dan:

> "Here is a test to find whether your
> mission on earth is finished: if you're
> alive, it isn't."

Dan certainly found a path through the fog of uncertainty that envelops the onset of retirement. Through it he found the perfect opportunity that matched his very unique skill set. A little prayer, a little effort, and maybe a little risk taking led him to where he could glorify God by utilizing his years of expertise and acquired wisdom.

Joe Salvagni – A Retired Police Officer and Youth Minister

Joe grew up wanting to live his life in one of two types of service —either as a police officer where his family had a long and rich history, or as a youth director fueled by the mentorship and love he treasured from a childhood pastor. He started college on the law enforcement path, but quickly reversed direction to pursue and eventually obtain his Youth Ministry degree. While at the university, he was able to go on several short term mission trips to Haiti. He fell in love with the idea of a servant's life, but ultimately felt he could best serve in law enforcement. So upon graduation from Kentucky Christian University, he reversed direction again, moved back to New York, entered the Police Academy, and graduated Top of Class. The thrill of being a police officer finally won out.

Joe thoroughly loved his law enforcement career and found great pleasure in serving his community. Then, one cold November night his professional life took its first dramatic twist. The dispatcher crackled the urgent message that there was an apartment complex for the elderly on fire. As the initial responder on the scene, he found the building fully engulfed in fire. With many elderly residents hanging from their balconies, he set up a rescue effort with a fellow responder that had also arrived on scene. As his partner climbed up to a third floor balcony, his large police flashlight fell the full three stories and struck Joe square on the head. He suffered a massive traumatic brain injury that changed everything.

While injured beyond what most would consider unrecoverable, Joe wasn't ready to capitulate on the career and work he loved so much. He was in the fight of his life but refused to give up. The next year was spent recovering and dealing with post-traumatic stress, incredible sensitivity to light and sound, and daily severe migraine headaches. After receiving a Medal of Honor for his actions, he fought both the pain and the odds to re-gain his position in the Police Department.

After a few additional years of service, on another cold New York night, he responded to another fire under nearly identical circumstances. This time he entered the building and rescued eleven people before succumbing to smoke inhalation. On his release from the hospital, all the memories, pain, and emotional stress came back with a vengeance. After being awarded his second Medal of Honor, the Department stunned him by demanding a medical discharge. He would never again serve as a police officer and was crushed.

After eleven years on the police force, he was abruptly told it was over. Giving his situation over to Jesus, he prayed for a miracle. The next year was spent helping a local church youth group, but he continued to pray diligently for his future. One day a friend asked if he wanted to join a construction team heading to the Dominican. He jumped on the chance to go on another mission trip, this being his first to the Dominican.

The team worked like crazy all week on a roof in the sweltering heat, but finished the job. On the next to last day there, he had his pivotal moment. Every day at the site the team brought bags of clean water to drink. As is commonly done, they stored them in a cooler with some ice. On this particular day a couple small boys saw that he was about to throw away the small amount of melted ice water and begged him not to. Through an interpreter, they asked if they could run home, a little over a mile each way, and come back with some containers to capture the ice melt. Joe came to learn that they hadn't had clean water in days and would do anything for the clean water he wanted to dump. That is the precise moment God grabbed his heart and he knew what he had to do with the rest of his life.

To know much and taste nothing; of what use is that?

- St. Bonaventure

Back home, an internet search quickly landed him at the Water@Work website. Joe knew he wanted to be a missionary to the Dominican Republic focusing on clean water and evangelism, but Water@Work at that time was not in a position to support its own missionaries. So doing the next best thing, he spent the next half year vetting many ministries and opportunities.

He ultimately decided on Score, International; a hugely impactful sports related mission organization in the Dominican Republic. His assignment was to develop a water plan for the communities they supported, and he quickly made his first trip in-country as their missionary. In only the way God can make things happen, our team happened to be in-country at the same time. A local partner educated us on Score and all the great work they were doing so, when asked if we wanted an introduction, we eagerly accepted. It wasn't even ten minutes after we entered their compound that we actually met Joe in person.

Since that time, our two organizations have teamed to build many Hub Site water plants. Score supplies construction mission teams and vetted sites where they work and know the community and pastor well, and we do our thing with the water plant. It is literally a partnership made in heaven.

Bobby Smith, Senior Pastor of Journey Community Church

Journey Community Church in Augusta, Georgia is a spirit filled congregation approaching 1,500 persons led by their charismatic pastor, Bobby Smith. Perhaps charismatic isn't an accurate or, more rightly, sufficient word. It doesn't take long to see that his very essence exudes the spiritual gifts of leadership and communications. Simply sitting in on the church's regular Monday morning staff prayer meeting is a testament to his gifts and compassion towards his congregation and mission work.

More than that, he can best be described as a visioneer; one that not only crafts a vision for his church, but then implements it with detail as an engineer would. It's also perhaps the best way to reconcile the dramatic growth of a church from its initial year only a little more than a decade ago.

I am greatly heartened by the church's foundational belief that their "community" includes all peoples in all lands. While every church would want to believe that they are as well, an examination of mission budgets would show a propensity towards local missions. Certainly Journey provides significant support to the local community and nearby missions, but it is their support for international missions that are extraordinary. It is a healthy mix that challenges its congregants to become truly engaged with both domestic and international opportunities to share the love of Christ.

Our relationship with Journey was actually initiated through the mutual support of John and Donna Bearden, the Dominican missionaries we have previously met. With both Journey and Water@Work supporting the Beardens, the development of a supportive relationship was natural.

Journey has since become an active supporter of Water@Work. They are representative of the many churches that form the backbone of Water@Work. In addition to financial sponsorship, there is also prayer support, hands-on visits in-country, and organizational mentoring. Not only does their staff help in our US-based efforts to raise awareness and be as professional as possible, but they moreover keep in close touch with our Dominican based teammates and their families.

I am reminded of one typical visit that was scheduled for half an hour with Pastor Bobby…that is, until we began talking and dreaming for both our organizations. Three hours later we had to break and return to reality. Oh well, just a great episode of visioneering with Pastor Bobby!

Charlie Gray, a Financial Advisor

Charlie is an old and dear friend that I only met a little over a year ago. Normally friendships that go a little deeper have been in the forming for many years. But that's the way it is with kindred spirits. It doesn't matter if we are navigating through the Dominican on their "suggested road lanes" or grabbing a quick meal together back home, his one and my one always equals three or more.

More than a good friend and great financial analyst, he seamlessly merges work skills with ministry to maximize his gifts to God. In military parlance, he is a force multiplier with his eyes set on kingdom building.

Charlie eagerly shares the tremendous satisfaction he gets from working with his ministry teammates towards God's glorification. But service in God's name is not exactly new to Charlie. He is a Partner and leader of an exciting financial services company that focuses on wealth generation for the purpose of enhancing donations to whatever cause really touches his clients' heart. He is blessed to advise people from all strata of wealth on ways to maximize their contributions to society and God, the very description of what he terms a "meaningful life." The goal of his work is of course increasing wealth, but it is wealth for the purpose of empowering the individual to be as impactful as they can. Any number of both faith and civic based causes are far better off because of his professional efforts.

His is a unique witness; his is a life driven to help others earn as much money as possible so that they can then gift it to charity. Many people have the natural desire to maximize their particular skill sets and earn as much as they can. Many additionally feel a sense of guilt in their building wealth while they see a world in need. Charlie makes clear the reality that making money need not be sinful. He works with his clients to get the most of what they make, and to then give to all types of charities for the betterment of society.

Helping others maximize their impact, as well as his personal involvement, has exposed Charlie to a great many causes. Water@Work has been new and different for him because of the international component. I was blessed to be the one to first expose him to life outside the resorts. Millions of people visit the Dominican every year to vacation at the beautiful beaches that surround the island. It is a shame that most only drive by the locals on their way to and from the airport. Nearly none of those vacationers will ever take a turn that leads to the heart of the country and the millions of brothers and sisters in need. Charlie describes this as his most difficult memory of working in the ministry.

"What then is Apollos? What is Paul? Servants through whom you believed, as the Lord assigned to each. I planted, Apollos watered, but God gave the growth."

1 Corinthians 3:5-6

On his Vision Trip, Charlie witnessed poverty that he knew existed but that he never had come face to face with before. Water@Work conducts at least two Vision Trips per year when we bring people in-country for an extended weekend to first experience bateys and communities in need, and then those that have been blessed with a water plant. The difference is startling and really drives home the value of the work done through the ministry. Too often it seems the focus is only on the need—picture after picture of the destitute. While integral to part of the story, it is not *the* story. It is eminently more important to elaborate on the second part of the story. This part embodies personal and community transformation. It is a focus on hopes and dreams realized, as opposed to the reiteration of a problem that has been around since biblical days.

We have found that there is a definite need to educate interested people on the problems we address. Spending twenty-five minutes on the problem and five on the solution won't cut it. Far more significant is the discussion of what happens after we do our work and then leave.

In this humble ministry, Charlie has found like minds serving for no other reason than to glorify God. And in his own words, he says that God has clearly shown him that even though he is just one, he can make a huge difference by the multiplying effect of the teammates and organization.

Ishani Chawla, an Elementary School Student

When Ishani was in the fifth grade, she was made aware of the lack of clean water in the world and wanted to help. As part of a school challenge, she was tasked with finding a project where she would "give herself away" to make the world a better place. Her choice was an easy one, and she immediately jumped on the clean water crisis. While not having access to anything more than that of a fifth grader, she set out to do the best she could with what she had. At first, she struggled to find something she could do as a child that would have an impact. She decided that she could hand-draw bookmarks and ask for donations in exchange for one.

At about the same time, the local community where she lives was having a Taste Festival where local restaurants come and sell small amounts of whatever type of food they are best known for. Ishani saw it as a perfect venue to "sell" her bookmarks. Over the coming days, she made many beautifully colored bookmarks. She then contacted the festival coordinators and was invited to come to the festival and hand out the bookmarks in exchange for a donation to Water@Work.

Although tired from a long day approaching strangers to donate money at the close of the festival, Ishani wasn't satisfied. Over the next few days, she went door to door in her neighborhood offering her bookmarks and asking everyone to donate. On the following Sunday, Ishani received permission from her church to give away the bookmarks in exchange for a donation. She excitedly took the opportunity to speak with dozens more people.

Altogether, Ishani raised more than $800 for Water@Work. This very significant amount was promptly combined with other donations to build a Water plant at a batey in need. Her efforts translated into the tangible benefit of bringing many families in the Dominican Republic clean and healthy water. Equally important is that many, many people were introduced to both Water@Work and the global water crisis through the process.

When we speak of trying to figure out how we can utilize our skill sets to make a major impact in the world, it may be best to follow the lead of this terrific child. Simply take God whatever you have and ask Him to multiply it. With Ishani, He took the love and creative talents of a small child and turned it into real blessings for many. We also took a great deal of pleasure in explaining to the community that received the Water plant of her story and how they had a fifth grade girl to thank for their future good health and prosperity. This in turn inspired the adults of the community to work hard to maximize the benefit, and her story was further used by them to inspire the children of the batey.

Tina and Byron Bradley, a Retired Couple

I have been blessed to know Tina and Byron for well over a decade. In that time they never cease to amaze me when it comes to their heart for missions and missionaries. It goes well beyond the fact that Byron has a brother that has served as a missionary in the Far East for his entire adult life. It also goes beyond their willingness to serve in such capacities as a Stephen Minister leader for their church and community, working in construction ministries, international child sponsorships and, of course, Water@Work.

As the years have progressed and their mobility reduced, they continue to provide many great missions with prayer and financial support, of which Water@Work is blessed to be one. Although retired and unable to travel to difficult environments, Tina and Byron feel a tremendous satisfaction in continuing to support as they can. They are a faithful example of finding a way to share Christ's love even though they must now be long distance partners instead of doers.

Limited mobility from a terrible car accident many years ago makes travel to the Dominican bateys or short term mission trips something Tina cannot experience in person. Despite physical limitations, she and Byron are nonetheless faithful in their support. With regularity, both she and Byron pray for our ministry and our team, as well as help to spread the word about the ministry and the clean water crisis.

Over coffee in their comfortable suburban Atlanta home, they passionately speak of *"feeling a need"* to support as they can. There isn't a specific cause or particular area of focus to their expressions of love, but rather their heart goes out to those whom they feel are honest in their commitments to serving Christ. They thrive on a connection with people in service rather than one cause over another.

Tina and Byron are a terrific example of doing what one can with what one has. Prayer and financial support are what sustains our ministry, and it is supporters like the Bradleys that enable us to do what we do. Just because one cannot physically participate in missions, any individual can still be a lifelong partner in mission through generous and regular prayer.

Life Lesson 17

What a blessing to witness so many people of differing backgrounds do what they can to serve Christ.

18. The Body in Motion

"Father, I pray that all people that believe in me can be one. You are in me and I am in you. I pray that these people can also be one in us, so that the world will believe that you sent me."

John 17:20-21

The word *praxis* usually refers to the process of putting theoretical knowledge into practice. However, the strategic and organizational usage of the word emphasizes the need for a constant cycle of learning from experiences for the purpose of reframing strategic and operational models. Praxis is also the point where our faith and our actions intersect. It is the point where what we believe and what we do join together based upon experience. To put it simply, praxis means walking the walk as well as talking the talk after prayerful reflection.

There has certainly always been that desire within Water@Work. Thousands of hours of prayer coupled with constant self-analysis and measurement have been invested by the many dozens of people we have met in this book, and the thousands more unseen. And within the framework of the organization one cannot help but be amazed at how the Body of Christ has been moved.

The result has yielded an international ministry that truly reflects the Body coming together to glorify Him. It is a refreshing endeavor to look back and see how so many disparate people and organizations have coalesced into one singular entity. It would be hard to think of any denomination that does not lavish extensive prayer support on Water@Work. Many Christian denominations have additionally provided funding or mission teams to both construct the community water plants and support the critical in-country operations.

Equally important to the many Christian denominations lending their support are the individual Christians that give so much. You have read in this book the stories of many of them, but the number that could not be in this book is staggering. Whether it be prayers, fund raising, the lending of specific talents at a time of need, or just spreading the word of what Water@Work is doing in the Dominican Republic, the variety of people from every walk of life that have left their impact is overwhelming.

The Power of The Body

Perhaps the effects of Christians coming together to spread the love of Christ through clean water and community development is so easy to see in Water@Work because there appears to be so much divisiveness in the world. The world in general and the Christian world in specific just can't seem to agree or come together on any subject.

The secular world is divided. Unity in any form seems nonexistent in our divided world. One can pick any subject and we will find a reason to be divided and, many times, violently so. Within our country, we find plenty of reasons to not get along with other races, cultures, family values, and so on. And when did it become the norm that when one is of a particular political party everyone that agrees with them are considered angels, and those from a different political persuasion are thought of as demons? The nightly news has become a regular liturgy of hateful expositions.

The Christian world may be slightly better, though we seem to have also found an incredible number of reasons to divide us. We won't even attempt to document the long list of issues that we find as reason to differentiate ourselves. From whether one gets drizzled or dunked in baptism to the treatment and message for the homosexuals in our community, nothing seems easy. Worst of all is that while we spend inordinate amounts of time debating nuances in theology, the enemy of our God keeps plugging away. Never tiring. Never taking a break. Just constantly creating and exploiting weaknesses in The Body.

And yet when people come together in Christian service, The Body never seems stronger. I have been blessed to see different denominations with serious differences work happily alongside each other. Perhaps that is the beautiful secret to international missions. For some reason, when we leave our borders we have a different perspective. All that counts are the masses of people in need of spiritual and physical saving. I have found that few in the developing world ever ask about the variations in denomination. They instead ask to know about Christ and, in doing so, convict all of us that hurt The Body through divisiveness. And to be completely honest, it is a whole lot more fun and satisfying to talk with people about the saving grace of Christ instead of the discussions that we regularly seem to get bogged down in.

Water@Work has only one litmus test for those wishing to serve in the organization: everyone must be a professing believer in Christ. That's it. Any denomination is welcome, but when we come together, it is to serve Christ. When traveling in-country, any personal essentials and gifts for those we serve is beneficial baggage. Any type of spiritual baggage can be left behind. The focus is on a collective of Christians representing our risen savior to people that don't know or want to know our differences. All the horses pulling one cart in the same direction with all their strength and capabilities. It's incredibly refreshing. Jesus came to this earth to bring people together and unite them. Who are we to do any different when we are supposedly representing him? Working in this manner produces a powerful Body indeed.

The Versatility of The Body

The Body of Christ coming together in international service is not only incredibly powerful from the perspective of unity, but from the variety of talents required to meet the needs of an international operation. As has been hopefully conveyed in this book, it took Christians of many different talents to create and grow Water@Work. Engineers, chemists, financial advisors, accountants, contractors, pastors, homemakers, logisticians, marketers, nurses, doctors, and virtually any other profession or vocation one can imagine has added critical input into the operation.

This diversity is paramount to an effective Christian ministry. As has been noted already, differences of opinion and passion for varying ideas are generally difficult to manage. After having been involved for a lifetime in both non-profit and for-profit companies, this double edged sword can either be used to slice through the tangled briar of issues or result in deep self-inflicted wounds.

From a positive perspective, competing ideas and passions generally lead to better decision making and well thought out movement. A room full of "yes men" has never produced anything but stagnation and a slow downward spiral. As General George S. Patton has famously said:

> "If everyone is thinking alike, then
> somebody isn't thinking."

Unbridled differences without effective leadership to discern and decide results in chaos and bad TV reality shows. Most people devoted to a non-profit as either employees, volunteers, or leaders have significant passion for the work of that organization. Why else would they sacrifice time, treasure, and talent for the cause?

Passion can unfortunately be like magnetism; it can simultaneously attract some while repulsing others. However, passionate people need not necessarily attract or repulse. With effective leadership they can instead complement.

There is a critical difference in the psyche of people involved in non-profits. That difference really comes from the infusion of love into the mix. Just as when two people in love have differing opinions, they generally (hopefully) unite into a single, better result. The only time this does not happen is when one feels the need to exert power over the other or when the goal becomes personal instead of family-centered.

The Body is no different. Differing parts of The Body can either be destructive or complimentary depending on their love and motivations. The versatility and expanse of talents represented by The Body are beautifully powerful. The full utilization of these resources falls upon the leaders in the organization.

Leadership Within The Body

If selflessness and the desire to express love triumph in both personal relations and ministry or church relations, it will always result in a strong Body and honest service to our Lord. Christ intends for His Body to consult with Him regularly and rely on His examples to be faithful to His desires for His ministries.

Effective leaders in non-profits learn early on to welcome and embrace differing viewpoints, but rely on love, discernment, a desire for unity and the optimum path forward.

Here is an additional truism on effective leadership in non-profits and ministries: the valuable leader nurtures and facilitates rather than leading in decisive terms. If one assumes that everybody participating in the organization is there for the love of the service being provided, whether internationally or locally, then the effective leader must cultivate complementary decision making.

A nurturing leadership style does not necessarily come naturally and must be developed. Jack Welch, the past iconic Chairman and CEO of the General Electric Corporation has stated this clearly.

"Before you are a leader, success is all about growing yourself. When you become a leader, success is all about growing others."

His perspective is spot on. But how much of this do we see in the world of non-profits? I would argue that in most, this is a rarity. Small non-profits generally lack the resources to accomplish both their mission *and* the need for "growing others". This becomes truer as the organization utilizes volunteers for more and important functions. Volunteers that may put in a few to a dozen hours per week and then go on to live their lives rarely benefit from nurturing leadership. Instead they become task doers. Necessary and gratefully accepted service, but ultimately relegated to an entirely follower situation.

While many welcome this or periphery service, it often drives professionals and management types that volunteer crazy. Those that are normally used to leading or decision making will eventually exit the non-profit where they feel their skills are not commensurately utilized. A true servant attitude will lead these people to assuredly serve, but they will ultimately tire and leave for an organization that better accommodates their gifts.

Small non-profits also suffer from simply not enough hands to keep all the proverbial juggling balls in the air. Not having enough human resources means that those involved need to do the jobs of many. There is simply not enough time to do all that needs done and still nurture the few involved. I suppose it could be argued that this was the situation with Water@Work in its first year or so, but the movement away from this was executed as quickly as possible.

Another typical leadership situation is seen in those that develop around a charismatic individual. A non-profit with a leader that makes all the decisions, is the face of the organization, and fully participates in the services provided can suffer badly when that person retires. Worse yet is the situation where the leader suddenly passes away. Is this the model provided by Christ in the gospels? It could be argued that the majority of Christ's time in His ministry was devoted to staff development. Additionally, how many non-profits, particularly small but true for larger ones as well, have a formal or developed succession plan? Yet in for-profit business, these are generally well conceived, understood and executed when necessary.

Larger non-profits are not immune. Many leaders in these organizations either come from the for-profit sector or have made the non-profit world a career. Often, they are chosen for positions of leadership in the hopes that they will bring a for-profit perspective to the non-profit in need of improvement. These individuals will often develop hierarchies to reflect efficient models in the for-profit sector. Unfortunately, many of these by their nature encourage competition among staff that can be destructive in non-profits.

Any person working within their career field will have desires for advancement. This is only natural and should be expected. Staff is most likely to continue serving the non-profit from a desire to share their love, but will constantly be tempted to exhibit all the characteristics of an employee looking to move up. Not all of this is necessarily bad; after all the drive to succeed is admirable. It's just that as with employees in the for-profit world, many negative or destructive traits can creep in.

Putting the Body of Christ in motion is absolutely the truest and purest method to affect change. After all, that's the way God designed it!

Life Lesson 18
No one organization, government, corporation, or non-profit can affect true change on country-wide basis. It takes the Body of Christ coming together in *unity* and humility seeking only to glorify God.

From the Random House Dictionary to you:

"*Unity*"
1. *the state of being one; oneness.*
2. *a whole or totality as combining all its parts into one.*
3. *the state or fact of being united or combined into one, as of the parts of a whole; unification.*
4. *oneness of mind, feeling, etc., as among a number of persons; concord, harmony, or agreement.*

19. From Small Things (Big Things One Day Come)

"Then I heard the voice of the Lord saying,
"Whom shall I send? And who will go for
us?" And I said, "Here I am. Send me!"
Isaiah 6:8

In reading this book, one might get the impression that Water@Work has it all figured out. We've been there and done that. Fortunately, nothing could be farther from the truth. On any given day, every topic discussed in this book could be in significant need of improvement or additional resources. And of course we have no idea what this ministry will look like going forward. Please don't be confused by the word "fortunately." Change and the evolving nature of life are inevitable. We have the choice to embrace it or run from it. If you would have felt more comfortable with me writing "unfortunately," you may wish to step back and ponder that a bit.

Certainly, change often necessitates a great amount of work and stress. But the reverse would be hard to imagine as better. Love is an action word, and actions lead to transformation. Deep down, nobody really wants to ever be a part of the status quo. And I would venture that despite the temporary negatives, most people at some level desire to be agents of change. After all, who would want to be a part of an organization that viewed its volunteers, staff, and customers as routine or part of the job and not as positive influencers and change agents?

Water@Work is hardly status quo, and is regularly evolving. Quite frankly, it is hard to imagine a time when we could even remotely feel comfortable with the way things were. In the vein of this uniquely American perspective, are we ever really satisfied with the way things are? People tell me all the time that they admire how, through God's grace and provision, Water@Work has affected so many.

Really? While grateful, I still can't seem to get past the faces of hundreds of thousands in the Dominican bateys still in need.

Traveling the globe has borne witness to the vast majority of people not only living in the status quo, but suffering through institutional apathy. It is painfully normal to see the common expectation that their lot or circumstances cannot change significantly. I regularly praise God because I live in a culture that encourages dreaming and action.

Of course, every so often it would be nice to turn it off. Even in those wonderful times of relaxation and quiet reflection, it still seems impossible to fully stop thinking about model improvements, capacity building, evangelism programs, funding needs, and on and on.

Gratefully, I am not alone in this preoccupation. Most everyone else in the organization suffers from the same condition, which then generally manifests itself in a lot of really great conversation and proposed ideas. The result is an organizational need to flush them out and, in some cases, implement them with the same limited staff and volunteers as were available before. As one might expect, a lot of promising initiatives never have the opportunity to fully take hold.

Engaging God's Angels

If you remember back a few chapters ago, we discussed the realities of capacity building. This is a daily issue for Water@Work, and one we regularly pray about. We are seemingly always in need of every type of human resource possible. Compounding the frustration is that while our operations are centered in the metropolitan Atlanta area, many people that want to engage with us are in a different geography.

Many thousands of short term missionaries from just about everywhere travel to the Dominican bateys or poor rural communities to work. In doing so, many come in contact with our water plants because of the team members' need for clean water and thereby learn about the ministry. When these missionaries go home to all parts of the United States and beyond, they share the good news of what they saw in the Water@Work water plants.

While many will try to raise the funds to place a water plant at the community church where they worked, many others will want to help the ministry with their personal talents. Their remoteness from our operations in the past made engagement difficult, and we certainly didn't want to "unwittingly turn away the potential angels among them."

The future and growth of Water@Work is directly proportional to its successful exposure throughout the United States.

In response to this situation, we developed specific opportunities for people that may never be able to work with us in Atlanta but that can still be critically helpful. Most of these efforts center on creating awareness within their local area. For example, one could become what we refer to as *Water Ambassadors*. These are people that become very knowledgeable on our model and goals, and then present the ministry to church and civic groups, or corporations and individuals that they feel would have an interest.

These Ambassadors take our message and share it with a host of fellow change agents wanting to do something about the clean water crisis, community development, and access to the gospel. This is just the ticket, for many want to do what they can to help build God's kingdom and share the love of Christ in a very tangible way.

Other areas exist as well, like conducting local golf outings, having a booth at community events, and any number of creative ideas brought by the individuals themselves. One may not be able to serve overseas or give a significant amount of time, but anyone can utilize their influence and time to make a difference. By representing our model and operations in a geography where we cannot, we are able to build that all-important capacity into our operations.

Dear God, Please Send Blessings ... and Directions

Perhaps the most exciting aspect of the ministry is that we really don't know where we are going. Water@Work can grow in many different ways depending on God's providence and its next generation of leaders. I have to admit that it is great fun to think about where the organization can go in the future! One thing is for certain – it will likely look different than today.

Given how much the model has adapted to the realities of the Dominican Republic, one can only expect it to do so again if the model moves to another country. Every country has its own realities concerning water and power availability, as well as types of water contaminants, government requirements, potential local support structure, the ability of the local residents to pay even a very small amount for the water, and many other issues.

> *Only God knows for certain the road map and paths to be taken in the future by Water@Work.*

And that assumes that the next move is to a different country. Another possibility is that it stays in the Dominican and moves away from the focus of the bateys and instead services the thousands of very poor barrios. Barrios are very similar to bateys, but they are typically home to documented Dominicans, and have full government representation.

They can be thought of as the working (or trying to work) poor.

While they are very much in need of a great many things, including affordable clean water, they have the blessing of being citizens and the protections afforded by the government. The communities are also a bit better off than bateys in nearly every criterion, and the church system is also stronger.

The benefit of staying in just one country is the already built Water@Work support structure, which may then additionally be utilized in these new communities. Plus, we have been carefully building a local brand built on high quality water at an ultra-low price. Staying in the Dominican can be thought of as the safe path.

Several key negatives also give rise to caution, perhaps the biggest of which is competition with the established water companies. Water@Work has always sought to pick communities that were not served regularly by any water companies, or at least reputable ones. It was never a goal to displace Dominican jobs by undercutting their product or pricing, assuming of course the water they provided was safe and reasonably priced.

Perhaps the road forward develops off-ramps into related and important avenues. With our customer communities we have begun extremely important ventures into food programs, industrial use of the clean water, liquid soap making and other associated extensions made possible by clean water. These Programs offer the expanding potential to fully exploit the clean water plant asset of the community.

Exciting outcomes from radical community transformation have already become evident. As an example, one of the communities that received a water plant a little over a year ago has launched a national evangelism program with its profits. They developed a praise band, funded the required music instruments, and purchased a bus to take the band on revivals throughout the country.

These and other efforts through the anointing of a mighty God can spread throughout the network of communities with water plants to truly "raise up" a strong and vibrant church in the country.

The bottom line is that the final chapters on Water@Work have not yet been written. What we've discussed in this book only reflects a few years leading up to, and a few years after, the initiation of Water@Work. Who knows what is coming? Things could indeed look very different in the future.

You could possibly be a part of that future. You may be the one that writes the next book on the next generation of Water@Work. And if not Water@Work, then perhaps some other great ministry that is poised for growth and just waiting for its capacity to match its vision.

Has Anyone Found that Road Map Yet?

Water@Work is like many wonderful organizations seeking to serve Christ and glorify God through the people that serve them. Any one of them is likely in need of people to fill specific gaps in its capabilities. Throughout this book we have been introduced to many people that have been critical to the success of the ministry. It is important to remember that the organization looks very different today than it did even a few short years ago entirely because of them. Together, they were the responsible parties that discerned the will of God for the organization and then plotted the course that was followed.

> *In the process of a person or organization doing something, it becomes something; whether it is for good or not.*

The truth is that no organization has a fully developed roadmap. The planning process can lay out a course and mitigate many bumps in the road. But if God is in the driver's seat, expect many turns to be taken. I simply pray that you find yourself a passenger in a vehicle that is perfect for you.

Hopefully you have thought the question "Am I fully using my talents to glorify God?" at some point while reading this book. Most Christians will wonder and ask themselves at some point if there might be more they could be doing with their time, treasure, and talent.

In our next and final chapter we will see that there is always room for you somewhere.

After all, God has thankfully designed his Body with a unique place for everyone that calls on Him for their salvation.

Life Lesson 19
Thank God we don't know the future, it would just ruin the surprise!

From Water@Work to you (as taken from its edited original documents):

The Vision *(the destination)*
To improve access to the Gospel of Jesus Christ and make a bold and lasting impact on an entire country's at-risk population by virtually eliminating water-borne disease and creating sustaining local businesses.

The Mission *(the reason for being)*
To mobilize brothers and sisters in Christ that then bring His message of hope to thirsty and at-risk people.

The Future *(the ultimate goal)*
To grow as God dictates and provides for, going where He sends us through the support of those He blesses us with.

20. If Not Me and You, Then Who?

"What good is it, my brothers and sisters, if someone claims to have faith but has no deeds? Can such faith save them? ... In the same way, faith by itself, if it is not accompanied by action, is dead."

James 2:14-17

One of the most loved miracles performed by Jesus while on earth, at least certainly by me, is the feeding of 5,000 men (an estimated 15,000 total people) with just two small fish and five loaves of bread. As someone that loves to go fishing on occasion, I assure you that quantity would be barely enough to feed just me and a fishing mate! There are so many lessons to be learned and interesting theological tangents to explore in this story. I'm sure there is a book somewhere that profoundly digs into all of these, but we will instead focus on one particular insight.

When Jesus looked up and saw a great crowd coming toward him, he said to Philip, "Where shall we buy bread for these people to eat?"[6] He asked this only to test him, for he already had in mind what he was going to do. Philip answered him, "It would take more than half a year's wages to buy enough bread for each one to have a bite!" Another of his disciples, Andrew, Simon Peter's brother, spoke up, *"Here is a boy with five small barley loaves and two small fish, but how far will they go among so many?"* Jesus said, "Have the people sit down." There was plenty of grass in that place, and they sat down (about five thousand men were there). Jesus then took the loaves, gave thanks, and distributed to those who were seated as much as they wanted. He did the same with the fish. When they had all had enough to eat, he said to his disciples, "Gather the pieces that are left over. Let nothing be wasted." So they gathered them and filled twelve baskets with the pieces of the five barley loaves left over by those who had eaten.

John 6:5-13

(Italics added for emphasis)

The thing that always sticks with me is that the miracle started with a boy stepping forward. I can't help but wonder how that exchange happened. *Um, excuse me Mr. Andrew, this is all I have. It's not much, but you can have it.* Did Andrew laugh at the illogicality of feeding so many with the small gift one boy could give? He clearly didn't have the faith that the offering of one small boy could make any significant difference.

Expect God's grace to work in and through you in miraculous ways when you let Him know all we have is His, even though it may not seem like much to us.

If we are being honest with each other, it is likely that any of us, myself for certain, would have thought the same. I could easily see myself as too embarrassed to volunteer my modest offering and instead assume that someone else with more resources would step up. His malady, secretly thinking we are not good enough, smart enough or perfect enough, has kept many from realizing the blessings that God had planned for them.

One of Christ's most illustrious miracles began with one modest person making a gift of the best he could offer. With this small measure and the blessing of our Savior, it was used to bring glory to God in a most incredible way. The same will occur with us if we let Him make it happen.

Just When You Though It Was Safe to Go to Sleep

At about the time I was fighting with God over the absurdity of someone like me starting a ministry in water purification, He spoke clearly and loudly to me. Everyone at some point has felt a heavenly nudge. This was nothing like that.

I woke up from a deep sleep with a simple expression clearly on my mind:

If not me and you, then who?

Even though the grammar isn't correct, that's it. This brief but entire message was thrown into my brain so powerfully that I got up and went to my home office to write it down. For many years I used it as my signature on every email I sent out. I wrote it in bold letters and taped it to the wall in front of my computer so I could see it all the time.

For a long time I used it as a conversation starter and point of departure for a discussion of my testimony. Later, at the onset of the ministry it became a rallying cry to get people to realize that if "me and you" didn't step forward in the small way that we could, like the boy in the miracle story, then who would? Even more importantly, if we assume God is the "me," and I am the "you," then there is a clear direction to rely on Him.

It's time to stop talking, debating and complaining, and time instead to rely on His leadership and provision to do something.

> *Even if you are on the right track, you'll get run over if you just sit there.*
> *- Will Rogers*

Learn, Earn, and Return

Many years ago, I came to realize that in a typical life duration of about 75 years, one experiences three fairly distinct and segmented periods or trimesters. These periods can vary in duration depending on every person's unique lifetime, but on average they each last about twenty-five years.

Learn:

In the first trimester of life we go to school and *learn*. While some of us may inject a little too much fun in the process, the primary outcome of this stage is the development of skills and personality to become fruitful members of one's family and society. It represents a significant investment from family, church, and society through schooling, nurturing, and oversight. The return on that investment can only be measured by the impact of the young person ultimately upon society.

Unless purposefully planned and watched over, young people can exit this stage with a significant emphasis on the self. Modern psychology tells us that it is developmentally natural for young children to be self-focused as they grow in their independence. However, wise guardianship ensures a conscious effort to help them realize their responsibility to the family and society that has raised them.

I feel a great sense of comfort from seeing many hundreds of youth at the Santo Domingo airport on Saturdays as they embark on a weeklong mission trip that will likely change their lives. Most will return home with a tremendous respect for the daily blessings we enjoy, and many will be led to give back to society through whatever cause God leads them to.

Earn:

The next trimester of life is the *earning* stage. Many here will enter service work either in the military or through many great non-profits, both of which I am incredibly grateful for. However, the vast majority will typically go into the workforce and try as diligently as possible to develop careers and stable, growing incomes. During this trimester many will scratch and claw and work as hard as possible to progress in the virtually unlimited number of trades and professions that embody our vast economy.

This can also unfortunately be the beginning of the great disconnect between those dedicated to service work and those pursuing careers in for-profit businesses. The two paths can be radically divergent, and the differences manifest themselves in many ways—from the perceptions and viewpoints that paint one's outlook to the friends one associates with. Studies show that some 85% of business people identify themselves as Christian. The tension between serving God and business requirements can unfortunately be high in many lives.

Over time, a dichotomy can develop that often reveals itself in ways that unfortunately hinder for-profit persons from participating in service work throughout this stage. Neither group here is wrong in their views. The way each sees an issue or challenge, as well as the method of decision-making is just generally very different. It can seem almost like a conversation in which the participants are speaking different languages.

I am reminded of four blind people in a room that are asked to describe an elephant that is also in the room with them. Each touches a part of the elephant and has very different perspectives of what the elephant looks like. The individual touching the trunk will see the elephant in a very different way than the person touching the leg, or the ear, or the tail; yet, all are describing the same elephant. Only through collaborative viewpoints can the elephant be effectively described. The corollary can easily be applied to successful ministry or non-profit work.

Return:

I am currently in the last trimester, or the *return* stage. Entry to this stage is always marked by significant change at a deep level. Things start happening when one hits their fifties and beyond that can be seismic in their affect. If one is blessed with children, they typically are off and starting their own lives. One may experience the passing of a parent or loved one. Many times the individual or their friends get serious illnesses. And it's hard to meet anyone in this stage whose knees or back don't remind them daily that their bodies are in decline.

All these, and the hundreds more not mentioned, cause the person to look back and reflect on their life and contribution. Advancing in a career can now seem more suited to the young turks that multiply exponentially with every year and never seem to run out of energy. It is also a time when many *return* to the community to share the wisdom earned after a lifetime of living.

"Whoever devotes themselves to themselves will have nothing but themselves to show for themselves."
Pastor Andy Stanley

USA Today conducted an exhaustive survey in January of 2015 concerning Baby Boomer retirement happiness. They reported that "about two-thirds (69%) say they had challenges adapting to this change in their lives. The toughest parts of retiring include missing the day-to-day social connections with colleagues (37%); getting used to a new and different routine (32%); and finding ways to give meaning and purpose in their days (22%)."

Yet the same survey also reveals that only 40% are volunteering at some level in non-profit or charitable organizations! With 59% of the total saying that their biggest issues with retirement are "missing the day-to-day social connections" and "finding ways to give meaning and purpose in their days", the math just doesn't add up. That gross discrepancy certainly draws a conclusion that there are huge numbers of retirees that would be happier if they just got involved with some worthy organization.

It's Just Not a Good Time Right Now

There are many lessons to be garnered from the review of life through the lens of Learn, Earn, and Return. Perhaps the most impactful however is that we all have certain age and skill dependent gifts that we can offer in service. No matter our age, we must all respect the efforts of society that gives us our chance to make things better.

Is it possible then to determine the best possible time within the three trimesters to be involved in service work? I would say an emphatic "NO!" Energy, knowledge, and wisdom can – and needs to – be shared at every stage of life. Imagine how God's kingdom could be advanced and society improved by simply recognizing that God is waiting for all of us to step forward with whatever gifts we have to offer.

No matter the age or condition you find yourself in, the Kingdom needs you. The servants we have met in this book come from vastly different circumstances, places, and backgrounds. Yet each has offered what time, talent, or treasure they could. Through the anointing of God, they have all multiplied their particular loaves and fish to make a huge difference for thousands in need.

Don't say you don't have enough time. You have exactly the same number of hours per day that were given to Helen Keller, Pasteur, Michelangelo, Mother Teresa, Leonardo da Vinci, Thomas Jefferson, and Albert Einstein.

H. Jackson Brown, Jr. (1940-)

Christ ended His time on earth and returned to Heaven after making the most important worldly contribution in history. I think every believer wants to emulate their Savior in their own lives as much as possible and exit this life knowing they have made a difference.

God doesn't create mistakes. He creates potential. Can you imagine the heavenly delight when that potential is used by the Holy Spirit to bring Him glory? We have been saved by Christ to be a blessing to others. This is the joyful, abundant life God promises us all. Yet the expectations of the world and the responsibilities of life often rob us of our inheritance.

It doesn't matter which life trimester one finds themselves in. The fallen world we occupy can often make our potential contribution seem too difficult to pull off or, worse, invaluable. Over a lifetime of self-indulgence and procrastination, the best way I have found to claim this better life is by simply and humbly bringing my bread and fish to the table God opens my eyes to.

If the appropriate table for you has not been apparent, then please pray for enlightenment. And please don't get discouraged if you get involved in some worthy activity that you thought was a good fit, only to find it disappointed you in some way. Anyone that has ever gone on a date knows that you sometimes need to dig a bit to get to the prize and find the one made for you by God.

Who Indeed?

So we end this chapter with the question that started it: "If not me and you, then who?"

And we end this book with my prayer that you realize that it has to be you. Only you, through the power of God, can solve the problems of the world, of your community, or of your neighbor.

May the Holy Spirit do with your prayer seed, gifts, and ideas what God does with the cherry tree in the springtime.

Life Lesson 20
No matter where I have been on my life journey there has always been a ministry that needed my time, talent, or treasure. I won't ever make the mistake again of being too busy to miss it.

From God to you:

    I love you.

    I need you.

    I'm waiting for you.

Acknowledgements

There are so many wonderful people that I would like to acknowledge for contributing to both this book and Water@Work. Throughout the book you have been introduced to dozens of such people, but there are many, many more that could equally share these pages. Each is treasured by the organization and me for all they do in His name.

The same can be said for my family and extended business family. Whether at home or the office, I can be sure to count on unconditional support and encouragement.

The Discussion Guide that follows however needs to have one special person individually acknowledged. Matthew Bullard, a very accomplished Christian Education Director, was kind enough and patient enough to co-write the Discussion Guide. We have been through a lot together, and his friendship is among my greatest treasures.

Discussion Guide ~ Part 1

Chapter 1 – Life Is Good

PERSON OF INTEREST:

Erven Kimble – Pastor, Professional Sales Person, Business Management

CHAPTER FOCUS:

It is very easy to find one's self in emotional, spiritual or professional ruts. While these ruts can make one feel secure, or even content, when in reality they impede us from engaging in new kingdom-based ventures.

- It is not necessary to uproot your life and devote all your time to ministry.

- The author discusses his reluctance to a full-time level of commitment, but exhibits a willingness to "start small".

- A significant first step is made with a decision to go on a short term mission trip through the local church.

- The single most important decision in life is living for Christ; not superficially like another rut, but with vigor to serve Him with the unique gifts He has given us all.

WHAT DO YOU THINK?

1. God has a specific purpose for every life He creates, including yours.

   Have you recognized your purpose or calling yet, and will you recognize it when it comes?

2. Just as God had a specific purpose and plan for Abraham, Moses, the apostles, etc, He has a purpose for everyone.

   What are some specific elements of His purpose and plan for you?

3. Moses was reluctant. Jesus repeatedly spoke to reluctant people.

   What makes you feel reluctant to follow your purpose or calling?

4. The author speaks of a reluctance to take a first step towards serving Him.

   What might your first step be?

5. If Jesus were to come back physically and walk up to you and say that he had something for you to do, you would likely do it.

   How is that different than responding to Him now?

Discussion Guide ~ Part 1

Chapter 2 – Marginal Importance

PERSON OF INTEREST:

Larry Wood – Retired Pastor

CHAPTER FOCUS:

It is easy to feel busy and unable to get involved in new activities, even those that glorify God. Make a decision to create free time for God to do something special in your life.

- There are many ways to increase your "time margin", and it is important to determine the optimum method for you to create more.

- If you are overly engaged and lacking available time, keep working hard at it to incrementally add a little more over time.

- If you are fortunate enough to have available time currently being filled unproductively, reduce those times and devote some of it to serving Christ.

- People that maximize their time margin find a better balance in their lives and are generally grateful for the conscious decision to do so.

WHAT DO YOU THINK?

1. The author makes a point of identifying the major tasks that take time and decrease available time for ministry, or what he refers to as time margin.

   What might be robbing you of margin?

2. Most Christians would agree that all of life belongs to God.

   How are you being a faithful steward of your limited time here?

3. All of humanity has twenty four hours in a day.

   Of that amount, how much do you spend in Christian service to those not related to you?

4. Service time does not need to be all or nothing and small efforts will lead to big returns and increased desire for more.

   In what ways can you add incremental time to service?

5. Many times we get involved in worthy activities and then never leave even after the critical difference you could make has been made.

   What are you doing that could be done by others? Is it time to quit something to make time for the purpose or calling God has for you?

6. Every person has skills; spiritual gifts that God has blessed you with.

   What are yours, and which may be of critical benefit to a ministry or non-profit in need.

Discussion Guide – Part 1

Chapter 3 – It All Began With a Mission Trip

PERSON OF INTEREST:

Antonio Feliz Gomez (Chaggy) – Dominican based mission team liaison and translator

CHAPTER FOCUS:

Everyone should absolutely take an international mission trip at some point in their lives to personally witness and experience both physical and spiritual poverty. According to UNICEF, half the world's population of children lives in physical poverty, and unmeasurable millions live in spiritual poverty. It will likely lead to an incredible stirring of the spirit and you will never be the same.

- International mission trips offer a tremendous insight into the challenges of serving Christ in different cultures.

- Getting your hands dirty can be a lot of fun!

- One has to actually go into the world to fully appreciate the difference in lifestyles and daily living endured by most people.

- The only way to understand the challenges people face in different countries is to be there and make it personal.

- God just may touch your heart when you put yourself among His children in need.

WHAT DO YOU THINK?

1. Most people have experienced poverty either personally or by witness in the United States.

   How do you believe that compares with the poverty experienced in the developing world?

2. The author speaks to providing construction assistance in the renovation of a local church, a typical church mission trip activity.

   What types of short term missions may be available to you in other areas of need (VBS, medical, etc.)?

3. When you think of going on a mission trip, particularly an international one, what feeling does that invoke (trepidation, excitement, joy, etc.), and why?

4. Have you had your spiritual "pivotal moment" in life yet?

   If not, is your heart truly and fully open to what He may want to share with you?

5. The author speaks to having a unique skill set in engineering and water science that served as the vehicle to see the opportunity God showed him.

   What unique skills has God specifically given you for the purpose He has for you to make a difference?

6. As you have probably encountered, there are many different types of mission trips focused on different results.

   Of those available to you, which ones might maximize your specific skills and interests?

Discussion Guide ~ Part 1

Chapter 4 – So What Exactly is a Batey?

PERSON OF INTEREST:

Moises Sifren – Hospital Administrator, Musician

CHAPTER FOCUS:

There are many difficult places in the world like bateys where survival is a daily exercise and Christ is virtually unknown. We must fight cynicism and the false assumption that there is nothing we can do. We instead need to recognize that we both can, and need to, empower lasting change.

- As you venture out of your comfort zone into His world, you recognize the tremendous blessings we have, and the tremendous needs of others.

- Some of the worst living conditions in the world are found less than a couple hours away from the United States in the bateys of the Dominican Republic.

- Even from the worst of conditions people can be brought up to affect significant change and become leaders within their own country.

WHAT DO YOU THINK?

1. We discussed in an earlier chapter the idea that while we have many resources, we have limited to no time margin. Yet in the bateys and rural Dominican communities the residents have ample time but no resources.

   How can this dichotomy be resolved?

2. The Invisible Poor that reside in the Dominican batey system go virtually unnoticed and have no safety nets or government protection.

   Can you think of any other population segment that could be thought of as invisible?

3. In this chapter we were introduced to Moises and his incredible story of survival and perseverance over desperate circumstances.

   If God can use one of these invisible poor in such a significant way, in what ways can God use you to further His kingdom and share His love?

4. The people and problems of the bateys, though in another country, are relatively easily accessible to those that are interested.

   What people in need make your heart "well-up" with compassion, and what would it take to access them regardless of their location?

Discussion Guide - Part 1

Chapter 5 – Everyone Gets a Mulligan, Right?

PERSON OF INTEREST:

Steve Flaim – Small Business Owner, Retired Coca Cola Vice President

CHAPTER FOCUS:

Very few people have everything all figured out. Just as in our spiritual growth journey, kingdom service needs nurturing, patience and faith. Even if you are uncertain how to proceed, just get started.

- It is easier to alter the path of a rolling ball than to get it started rolling, so get involved in any way possible and let God alter your path as He wants.

- It's easy to do long term harm when you are just trying to instead do good.

- All mission work should be driven by long term benefits for those being served even though short term objectives are often easier.

- Never give up on a calling from God when the world works against you - because if you are fulfilling His will, it most assuredly will.

WHAT DO YOU THINK?

1. Everybody experiences failures at some point, even when
    trying to help.

    What have been some faith based efforts you experienced
    that you would consider less than successful, and how has
    God used those in your faith journey?

2. The author makes a point that even in charitable works that
    may not exactly work out for you, you should not give up.

    Have you ever been involved in ministry or non-profit
    support work and felt unsuccessful or less than fulfilled? If
    so, how might God be starting a new work from the ashes of
    that effort?

3. You have experienced many non-profits and ministries from
    a distance, and may have participated at some level with
    them.

    Based on those experiences with these types of organizations,
    how could your involvement increase the success of their
    work?

4. Have you ever been tempted to compromise the centrality of
    Christ to achieve success, even in charitable efforts?

5. It seems paradoxical, but many times the best way to learn
    and grow is by failing at the things we try to achieve.

    What lessons has God taught you through the "failures" of
    your life?

Discussion Guide - Part 2

Chapter 6 – Caution, Objects in the Mirror May Appear Larger than They Are …

PERSON OF INTEREST:

Tim Fenbert – Financial Analyst, Insurance Sales

CHAPTER FOCUS:

Past mistakes are merely reference for a better future. Keep the end goal in mind always, seek Godly guidance and keep moving forward with your best efforts.

- Passion and energy can make up for a lot of mistakes and lack of resources.

- A business plan or strategic plan is important for entrepreneurial non-profits.

- Defining what success looks like for a particular endeavor is critical to any Plan.

- "Backward Think" is important to ascertaining past issues, identifying lessons learned and addressing any particular realities.

- If you are centered on the will of God, expect the enemy to struggle mightily to derail your efforts.

WHAT DO YOU THINK?

1. Who is the most impassioned individual you know, and what drives their passion?

   Is there anything or cause that gets to you?

2. Many people have experienced entrepreneurial efforts, though not necessarily in business, such as starting a Girl Scout cookie drive or charity golf event.

   Have you ever been involved with such efforts that could have benefitted from advance planning?

3. Everybody can look back on life and identify short comings.

   How have you learned from them so that the past becomes prolog for you?

4. Prolog has been defined as setting the stage for the next act; history is more of a remembrance.

   Would you consider your life issues prolog or history?

5. Tim was open to God's leading even in the course of a business lunch, and was looking for opportunities where God could utilize his gifts.

   Are you alert to the prompting of the Holy Spirit in the course of your day where you might say "maybe I can help"?

6. The author states that when we get involved in ministry, the evil one will do his best to derail our efforts.

   How have you experienced this in your life?

7. The author states that his issues always pale in comparison to the conditions and issues of the people he serves.

   How do you keep your troubles in perspective and maintain a healthy outlook?

Discussion Guide - Part 2

Chapter 7 – Water@Work Breathes at Last

PERSON OF INTEREST:

Robbie Gring Campbell – Marketing Consultant

CHAPTER FOCUS:

Entrepreneurial non-profits take huge amounts of nurturing and God needs to be in it for any chance at success.

- The best approach, particularly when first starting, should be to share your passion with everyone you meet, while allowing the Spirit to prompt people to become engaged.

- Maintaining a product mentality within a non-profit organization ensures a meaningful customer focus that consistently meets the needs of those you serve.

- A clear value proposition that can be easily and quickly articulated to interested parties helps get potential volunteers and donors excited about the opportunity and chance of success.

- Metrics of success are key to faithful stewardship and continuous improvement.

- Branding is just as important to non-profits as it is in for-profit organizations.

WHAT DO YOU THINK?

1. Many times we are tempted to persuade persons to be a part of something important to us, even when it may not be a good fit.

   Why do we attempt to push the process rather than let God lead people to us?

2. A product mentality is often discouraged in non-profits.

   What are some temptations that distract us from consistently providing what the customer needs?

3. An outside perspective of Water@Work would identify the local resident (end recipient) in the batey as the customer, when in reality the facilitator (batey pastor) and support structure (donors) are also considered as customers.

   Has your cause clearly identified and prioritized its customer types, and are the realities of the budget, time involvement, etc. appropriate for each year after year?

4. Hard metrics help articulate the success of any charitable effort or organization.

   How do you determine the success metrics or measurements for your cause?

5. The best run organizations have clearly identifiable and recognized brands.

   Has your cause developed a brand that resonates with all your customer types?

Discussion Guide ~ Part 2

Chapter 8~Organizational Development at Home

PERSON OF INTEREST:

Patrick Borders – Writer, Industrial Engineer

CHAPTER FOCUS:

Organizational development is critical and takes time, but God will provide the perfect people according to His plan.

- Organization charts are generally dull and done in reaction to a need, where they should instead be the first dynamic identifier of human resource needs.

- A positive systemic Christian culture throughout the organization will help you endure and sustain through virtually any circumstance.

- It pays to spend as much time as possible on identifying empty boxes in the organization chart, and then pray diligently for God to provide the perfect person according to His vision for your organization.

- Any "who" question should be answered by a box in the organization chart.

- Expect an early-stage non-profit organization to change many times to meet unfolding realities.

WHAT DO YOU THINK?

1. While organization charts are a necessary evil, they can yield clear direction on human resources and what to pray for.

   Is your cause's organization chart top down or bottom up, and how could it better serve your cause?

2. If you could no longer pursue your current career track, is a new path in charitable services a possibility? Would an income, even at a reduced level, make a difference?

3. The subject of the chapter, Patrick, felt a discontent and just seemed to know that he could be doing more with his life.

   Are you content with where you are in your life right now, or is God perhaps leading you to something else?

4. The author speaks to the importance of personal connections that motivate and nurture the all-important passion to serve.

   How are you putting yourself in situations where you can make personal connections with people in need?

5. The author states that *"the best people we can have involved are called by God, and may not have the earthly resume one would expect"*.

   Have you ever felt led to serve, but then didn't because you felt either over-qualified or under-qualified?

6. Organizational culture defines inter-personal professionalism.

   How are the characteristics of Christian culture different, and how would you infuse them into any type organization.

7. The word "Christian" defines is a wide spectrum of believers with differing theological perspectives.

   Are you able to have a constructive dialog with fellow Christians that disagree with you, and work from a spirit of grace? Have you ever been in the minority among fellow Christians and then been supportive of the ultimate decision?

Discussion Guide - Part 2

Chapter 9 – Organizational Development in the DR

PERSON OF INTEREST:

John Bearden – Public Servant in Wildlife Management, Law
Enforcement

CHAPTER FOCUS:

In-country operations are very different from what one expects
and require healthy doses of both patience and resources to
properly develop.

- Developing an organization in a foreign country can be
  frustrating beyond measure. Expect it.

- Cultural awareness, even in domestic ministries, requires a
  sensitivity the context in which you seek to help.

- Communications in foreign countries can be particularly
  challenging, both in terms of its availability and its quality.

- A strong in-country leader is absolutely necessary for success.

- Due to education levels, communications issues, illiteracy,
  and other maladies, expect the need for more human
  resources in international efforts than in domestic operations.

- Local people should be utilized for every need whenever
  possible to provide local jobs and valuable local perspectives.

WHAT DO YOU THINK?

1. Working in foreign cultures and lands has unique issues.

   What frustrations have you experienced working in a culture that did not necessarily represent yours?

2. Cultural sensitivity to things like poverty, language, customs, government, etc. is essential in any ministry wherever it works.

   What are the ten most important cultural elements that you should be sensitive to in your cause?

3. Properly implemented ministries learn how to communicate best within the paradigm of their service, including such areas as interpersonal conversation, appropriate dress, lack of telephony, electronic media, etc.

   In your ministry context, what are the obstacles to your effective communication with the people you are trying to serve?

4. Even in domestic ministries, every organization must rely on "boots on the ground" leaders that are physically at different geographies from the headquarters.

   What are the essential qualities and personality characteristics for the on-site leadership of your ministry?

5. It is vital to fill as many roles as possible with qualified local persons from where you operate.

   In your cause, what are you doing to ensure that your leaders and support persons appropriately represent the local community or country where you serve?

Discussion Guide - Part 2

Chapter 10 – Every Instrument Needs Regular Tuning

PERSON OF INTEREST:

Brandon Harper – Communications and Marketing

CHAPTER FOCUS:

Constant self-analysis and re-engineering is difficult and tiring but keeps organizations mission driven, viable and healthy.

- For-profit businesses have learned over the years the value of hard self-analysis and introspective endeavors, and so should non-profits.

- Continuous improvement is a non-profit responsibility to ensure faithful stewardship of gifts as the realities of the organization and those served change.

- The amount and variety of work effort involved in starting up a ministry is incredible and should not be under-estimated.

- Customer perceptions of your product and value proposition, in our case the taste and cost of the water, will dictate success more than anything else.

- Going "out-of-house" for solutions to problems is worth the risk of exposing weaknesses or issues.

WHAT DO YOU THINK?

1. It is incumbent on each person serving an organization to take it upon themselves to offer constructive feedback.

   What steps are you personally taking to critically review and better the organization where you serve?

2. Just as donors are faithful in their stewardship, non-profits have an even greater responsibility to steward the gifts they receive.

   How can you measure stewardship in the context of continuous improvement?

3. We often learn more from our failures than successes.

   What have you ever started, either personally or professionally, and what have you learned from the effort that can be applied to your ministry or non-profit endeavors?

4. To ensure success, one has to be certain that your customer sees what you have to offer as appropriate and valuable.

   What are some ways to make sure you and your organization are truly "connecting" with your customer and their real needs?

5. It can be difficult to discuss challenges a non-profit faces with people outside the organization for fear of exposing weaknesses or shortcomings.

   How can you assure there is a level of openness in your non-profit to solicit potential improvements, even from outside the organization when warranted?

Discussion Guide - Part 3

Chapter 11 – The Water@Work Model

PERSON OF INTEREST:

Mark Montonara – Communications Consultant

CHAPTER FOCUS:

The Water@Work model is truly unique and a different paradigm in developing healthy communities and individuals.

- Concise vision statements must feed correspondingly concise operational statements.

- The Water@Work model for service was developed to parallel the way Christ served the poor and needy while he was on earth.

- The complexities of the model are wrapped up into the simple concept of dirty water to clean water, clean water to living water.

- The radical sustainability component of the model can only be successful through an exceptional in-country support organization.

- The model for any international ministry must adapt to the cultural sensitivities of the particular country and people served.

WHAT DO YOU THINK?

1. Vision and Mission Statements by their nature are lofty and global when for operational implementation they need to be concise and specific.

   Synthesize an operational equivalent (such as Dirty Water to Clean Water to Living Water) for your cause in ten words or less.

2. Christ typically ministered to the physical needs of the individual and then to their spiritual needs.

   How closely does your service model mirror the model Christ set forth in the gospels?

3. Sustainability of whatever service or products an organization provides is critical to faithful stewardship of gifs and donations.

   What assurances do you have that your efforts and use of funds will remain operational and relevant for future generations?

4. Cultural sensitivities extend beyond how one operates and communicates within a foreign country or region, and affects the actual model for service delivery employed.

   Aside from being sensitive to speech, attitudes, mores and such, how do you ensure that the model for your service or product delivery reflects the cultural environment?

Discussion Guide - Part 3

Chapter 12 – Just One More Tweak to the Model

PERSON OF INTEREST:

Pastor Vilorio – local Dominican batey pastor

CHAPTER FOCUS:

The customer may not always be right, but they must always be the first opinion sought in effective service delivery and organizational planning.

- The effort of working with the local governing authorities is ultimately worth the exceptional amounts of time and frustration.

- Even the best of models can be improved, and it is incumbent on everyone in the organization to look for opportunities to do so.

- Non-profits should selectively seek business solutions to issues where appropriate.

- It is almost impossible for non-profits providing a service to at times avoid subtle attitudes of superiority, which should be actively identified and eliminated.

WHAT DO YOU THINK?

1. All governments have developed bureaucracies for the benefit of their constituents that can also be cumbersome and onerous to work within.

   Do you find the governing bodies where you work to be friend or foe, and what can you do to gain their favor?

2. Proactive and constructive challenges to a model are healthy.

   How are you empowering everyone in your cause at every level to actively look for ways to improve the model?

3. Many times the business community is considered an alien paradigm to non-profit undertakings and philosophy.

   What are you doing to engage and solicit solutions from the for-profit business community for your non-profit challenges?

4. It's almost impossible to not at times feel like all solutions to challenges should come from us because we so greatly want to help, and because we have so many resources readily available.

   What are you doing to foster an attitude of humility and inclusion with your clients and customers, and are you actively providing them with a proactive feedback mechanism?

Discussion Guide ~ Part 3

Chapter 13 – Meeting Customer Expectations

PERSON OF INTEREST:

Pastor Alejandro Guzman

CHAPTER FOCUS:

Whether delivering a product or service, an organization needs to identify all their customer types and their resulting expectations.

- The end user or service recipient is the most important customer, which for Water@Work is the batey or community resident.

- The community church pastor is the "middle-man" in the Water@Work model, and has entirely different expectations for service and product.

- The last type of customer is the donor organizations and individuals whose expectations rest on faith and accountability.

- Technology can be used to communicate with all customer segments, but personal involvement is critical to meeting expectations.

WHAT DO YOU THINK?

1. Identifying the ultimate recipient of your service is essential.

   Who is your most critical customer, and how do you ensure appropriate levels of communication?

2. Many times there are persons or organizations outside your own that become critical to the delivery of your service or product.

   Have you identified any for your cause, and how are you keeping them fully engaged and feeling like a vital part of your cause?

3. Every non-profit exists only through the generosity and satisfaction of a donor network.

   Do you consider persons or organizations that provide you gifts and donations as customers, and what specific methods do you employ to keep them informed and enthusiastic?

4. Technological advancements continue to change the way and frequency that we as individuals and organizations communicate with each other.

   How do you ensure that the appropriate communication method is selected to match that preferred by your customer?

Discussion Guide ~ Part 3

Chapter 14 - Meeting Accountability Expectations

PERSON OF INTEREST:

Gary Jones

CHAPTER FOCUS:

Accountability extends to all segments of the model, including the end customer in country and donors back home.

- Vague accountability leads to frustration and additional questions and requirements.

- Accountability must extend beyond donors or grant requirements. Respect for in-country end customers and local distribution through church leaders demands accountability to them.

- Accountability back to the organization is best served through the reporting of captured hard data and subsequent analysis.

- Having dedicated staff focused solely on accountability will result in the attention and quality it deserves.

WHAT DO YOU THINK?

1. Specific accountability results in an informed constituency and efficient operations.

    As a donor, how have you experienced vague accountability, and how did you feel about the lack of sufficient or appropriate communication? As a mission provider, how has vague accountability impeded your efforts to communicate effectively?

2. The essence of mutual accountability is true partnership.

    If you are the recipient of blessings from an organization, what types of measures can be taken to ensure the organization is aware and responsive to your specific needs?

3. Accountable relationships require effective communication from those you serve.

    What types of metrics are consistently received from the end recipients of your service so that effective analysis is possible?

4. An investment in a dedicated accountability person will pay immediate and lasting dividends.

    What differences have you experienced in working with organizations that either do or don't employ a dedicated accountability person?

Discussion Guide - Part 3

Chapter 15 – In-Country Partners

PERSON OF INTEREST:

Christin Hamner

CHAPTER FOCUS:

In-country partnerships are helpful because they can provide additional resources or cultural acceptance. Ultimately it serves the kingdom best for these relationships to be deep and lasting. Unfortunately because each party tends to guard its resources and contacts, developing these relationships can be challenging.

- Partnerships among organizations are difficult, and those among non-profits in foreign countries are the most difficult.

- Senior or managerial level staff located in-country will nearly always feel a lack of empowerment from the non-profit leadership in a different country.

- Cultural realities and operational differences can hinder effective partnerships with foreign entities

- Necessity often drives local partnerships instead of strategic synergies.

- While extremely difficult and always changing, the local government should be engaged with and welcomed as a partner.

WHAT DO YOU THINK?

1. It is reasonable for people to protect the resources and relationships that have likely spent years develop.

    How have you seen an inability to work well with another organization, even when you thought it positive for both?

2. It is all too common to experience different organizations with obvious synergies not working together.

    Why do you think it can be so difficult for organizations in the business of serving our Lord to work together effectively?

3. Failure to empower in-country senior staff leads to stagnation and lethargy in the operations.

    What can your organization do to ensure in-country senior staff is empowered to make appropriate decisions?

4. Sensitivity to local culture is critical because it can be impolite or even inappropriate to raise an issue or question anything put in place or offered by others. The American tendency to be assertive in decision making can exacerbate this problem.

    What are some ways to make sure local staff are encouraged to speak frankly and embrace being a valued part of a team?

5. Organizational synergies and mutual benefit lead to effective long-term partnerships.

    What are your experiences in partnerships that were synergistic and mutually beneficial? How did you avoid the pitfalls from a relationship that only benefited one party?

6. Local government officials with an influence over your operations can be an unpredictable, yet still critical partner.

    How are you cultivating a positive relationship with the local government where you operate, even if you serve in America?

Discussion Guide ~ Part 3

Chapter 16 – Home Based Partners

PERSON OF INTEREST:

Joe Burns

CHAPTER FOCUS:

Partners at home are critical to raising resources and awareness for the organization, but they need to be encouraged, cultivated and nurtured.

- Developing home based partners is difficult when the focus of the service is oversees or with a group that is difficult to relate with. Additionally, donors generally give more freely when they can empathize with the end recipient of the service or goods.

- There can be terrific alliances executed at home that extend the donor pool through common end customers and synergistic needs.

- Volunteers should be thought of as partners, and not staff.

- Mission teams from US churches provide an excellent extension of labor, and reinforce the organizations message that Christ cares about those being served.

WHAT DO YOU THINK?

1. The author discusses regional cultural conditions, such as daily survival in the Dominican batey system where people are generally thought of and treated as disposable, as opposed to America where every individual has dignity and worth.

   What are some effective mechanisms to evoke empathy with potential donors and volunteers for the culture you serve when conditions are so foreign to their personal experiences?

2. The goal of any non-profit or ministry should be to meet the needs of its constituents. However organizational tendencies can be territorial and protective, and not in their best interests.

   How can you personally be the agent of change that seeks out and establishes synergistic partnerships with others?

3. Treating volunteers as staff can lead to unreasonable expectations and burnout.

   How is your organization creating a culture that recognizes its volunteers as partners?

4. Water@Work benefits greatly from mission teams from America seeking construction projects in the developing world as an example of a positive synergistic partnership.

   What are some potentially synergistic partnerships that could help you better serve those you are called to?

5. Few Americans are truly aware of conditions in the developing world, and some have studied or spent time learning about the issues; however personal interaction in-country leads to a deeper awareness and empathy.

   How can you move donors to a deeper connection and empathy if they are unable to witness the needs in person?

Discussion Guide ~ Part 4

Chapter 17 – Stories From the Front Lines

PERSONS OF INTEREST:

Donna Bearden – a Nurse
Dan Blevins – a Retired Chemist
Joe Salvagni – a Retired Police Officer
Charlie Gray – a Financial Advisor
Bobby Smith – the Senior Pastor of Journey Community Church
Tina Bradley – a Retired Homemaker
Ishani – an elementary school student

CHAPTER FOCUS:

A variety of people and skill sets have come together to grow Water@Work benefitting not only the organization, but the individuals themselves.

- No matter what your skill set or background, a non-profit like Water@Work can use your help.

- It takes a variety of perspectives and involvement for an organization to be its best.

- If God has put a cause on your heart, then follow that lead and give time, talent or treasure as you are able.

- One does not need to physically go to the source of need, whether internationally like the Dominican or to a homeless shelter across town, to help.

- Those that cannot go can give prayer and financial support.

WHAT DO YOU THINK?

1. Everyone has value and something that they can do to benefit a non-profit or ministry building it capacity and operations.

   How can your specific gifts and talents be maximized to glorify Christ while meeting the needs of the world?

2. A diversity of opinions and perspectives is critical to effective leadership and operations in organizations, as it keeps them from becoming myopic and entrenched in decision-making.

   How can ensure that your cause is as effective as possible by utilizing and cultivating a multiplicity of perspectives?

3. Every Person of Interest encountered in this Chapter has had their heart opened to the ministry, albeit in different ways and for different aspects of the ministry.

   What are some tangible ways you have responded to God's call to service in your life?

4. Every movie has lead actors, supporting actors and those responsible for production.

   From a ministry or non-profit perspective, where have you traditionally participated and are you willing to participate at a different level from your traditional role (a lead actor serving behind the scenes in the nitty-gritty of production, or a supporting actor moving closer to a "front line" position)?

5. Prayer is the keystone of every ministry, and financial support is the mechanism for change.

   What are some ways to equip and inform prayer servants so that they may pray specifically for the needs and challenges faced by your cause, and to motivate donors to be more prayer conscious?

Discussion Guide ~ Part 4

Chapter 18 – The Body in Motion

PERSONS OF INTEREST:

All of Us – the Body

CHAPTER FOCUS:

The Body of Christ is the most powerful force on the earth when mobilized in unity to glorify God.

- The Body is and has been instrumental throughout the life of Water@Work.

- Engaging the entire Body of Christians and establishing respectful tolerance of differing Christian perspectives is the best way to unleash the true power of the Body of Christ, and ultimately leads to better discernment and decision making.

- Maximizing the power and versatility of the Body requires leadership that is characterized by facilitation; encouraging both organizational and personal nurturing.

- A significant impediment over the long term can be the charismatic leader through which the organization is identified, instead of the organization itself.

WHAT DO YOU THINK?

1. Water@Work has sought to integrate every aspect of the Body of Christ in its organization and operations.

    What are some ways to ensure your ministry fully taps into the power of the Body?

2. There is a continuum of theological perspective among Christians ranging from very liberal to very conservative, yet God's purpose for transformation is not divided.

    How can your organization stay focused on God's purpose and remain tolerant when deeply held convictions can cause differences of opinion? How have you witnessed diversity of perspectives ultimately lead to better decisions?

3. Command style leadership in ministry is ineffective at maximizing the full potential that is the Body of Christ.

    What are some ways that you can be the nurturing conduit that creates unity in your mission (for the sole purpose of glorifying God), while respecting a diversity of theological views?

4. There are many great ministries that are identified almost exclusively with one key person, and not necessarily the work that the ministry does.

    How have you seen this manifested, and how can you ensure that with the eventuality of a key person's departure the ministry does not suffer?

Discussion Guide - Part 4

Chapter 19 – From Small Things (Big Things One Day Come)

ORGANIZATION OF INTEREST:

Water@Work

CHAPTER FOCUS:

Water@Work is still young, growing and uncertain. The future begins with every new day, and will be determined by persons likely unknown to us now but already selected by God.

- Water@Work is continually evolving and growing to best meet the needs of its constituents; relentlessly working to avoid status quo.

- Organizational capacity building outside the geographic home area of a non-profit is crucial to long term health and diversity of support.

- The Water@Work Water Ambassador Program is a worthy example of long distance capacity building and volunteer engagement.

- With continued anointing and blessings from God, Water@Work will achieve its initial mission at some point in the future, but its next phase has yet to be illuminated.

- The exciting truth is that it is great to not have all the answers or the final road map.

WHAT DO YOU THINK?

1. A truly old business tenet is simply "grow or die"; meaning in part that an organization that is not growing its personnel, capacity or product or service offerings is, in fact, dying.

   How do you feel this applies, if it does, to the non-profit organization or cause that you care for deeply?

2. Many non-profits survive on a limited number of supporters and advocates that extend from the personal and professional networks of the persons involved in the cause.

   What are some ways that a non-profit can reach beyond this finite number to additionally engage diverse people of different backgrounds, perspectives and talents?

3. The author discusses how Water@Work attempts to engage interested persons from places far from their operations.

   Can you discuss three opportunities to engage volunteers that are geographically distant from your operational hub?

4. Water@Work can envision a time when it will have either achieved its stated mission or a significant measure towards it.

   Think of some examples of mature non-profits that a) cannot seem to grow to the next level, or b) cannot seem to fully achieve their vision. How might sincere focused prayer lead to Godly direction and success beyond their expectations?

5. Every non-profit or ministry at some point questions where its future donors, volunteers and staff will come from, often leading to organizational anxiety.

   Have you found yourself worrying about your causes' future, or do you place your trust in a sovereign God and enjoy the inevitable ups and downs, twists and turns?

Discussion Guide - Part 4

Chapter 20 – If Not Me and You, then Who?

PERSON OF INTEREST:

You – the Reader

CHAPTER FOCUS:

Only you, through the power of God and the leadership of the Spirit can solve the problems of the world, of your community, or of your neighbor.

- God is counting on us to step forward with our gifts, just like the boy in the miracle story when Christ feeds the thousands with two fish and five loaves.

- "If not me and you, then who?" can be a launching point for a ministry involvement conversation between both you and another person, or between God and you.

- "Learn, Earn and Return" is a concise perspective on life's three stages, and challenges the individual to be involved in service work at every stage.

- The best time to be involved in service work or ministry is now, regardless of the life stage or circumstances that one finds themselves in.

- God created each of us with a potential to make a significant difference for Him through the Holy Spirit.

WHAT DO YOU THINK?

1. The gospels are replete with stories of ordinary people stepping forward in a small way that are then multiplied by Christ in unimaginable ways.

   What small measure of time, talent or treasure can you offer that will bring Him glory?

2. It can be very easy to fall into a cynical attitude as we travel our journey, expecting others to do the labors of love that we are compelled by our Savior to partake in.

   What are some ways that we can always be on the watch for those special opportunities created especially for us?

3. Many times it is hard for us to see ourselves within the perspective of the different stages of life that we go through.

   How can you stay cognizant of where you are, when you are transitioning between stages, and the responsibility you have to serve both our neighbor and our Lord at all times?

4. The responsibilities and distractions of the world, and our reactions to them, make it easy to defer opportunities to serve or support ministry till later.

   How can you ensure that you always have an open heart to the prompting of God?

5. The world can make us feel anything but special by telling us that we are never good enough, talented enough, attractive enough, or possessing enough "stuff".

   Do you feel special to God; special enough that He would entrust something important to Him with you? What is it, and what are you waiting for?

About the Author

THIRSTY FOR CHRIST represents the first book by Tom Flaim, a business leader and noted speaker commonly known of as "the water guy". He is a graduate civil engineer from the University of Illinois and participant in the Master of Science in Management and Organizational Development Program at Benedictine University in Lisle, IL. As a repeat entrepreneur he has successfully started and grown several businesses. His latest is centered on water purification, and he has two patents pending for his pioneering technology.

His desire to serve Christ in all his efforts has focused his passion for clean water to serving in the developing world. This becomes readily apparent after learning about Water@Work, the ministry he founded, where clean water and living water come together to radically transform communities in need.

He has also personally deployed water purification technologies across Africa and North and South America in response to many dozens of natural disasters such as earthquakes, hurricanes and regional wildfires. Because of his experiences, he is a sought after speaker on these issues and has addressed or keynoted gatherings that range from church groups to large conventions. Being recognized internationally for his efforts, he has been interviewed or appeared on radio, television and print media as a unique expert on both international disaster response and the provision of emergency water.

To engage Tom Flaim to
speak at an event or to contact
him, please visit:

www.tomflaim.com

To learn more about
Water@Work, please visit:

www.wateratworkministry.org